Aim High,
ACHIEVE MORE

Napoleon Hill (1883–1970), best known for his global bestseller *Think and Grow Rich*, was a self-help author and businessman whose work has influenced millions across the world, from Norman Vincent Peale to Donald Trump. Born poor, Hill lived a colourful life, pursuing several different business ventures and professions. He also met and advised many famous people, such as US President Woodrow Wilson. Hill eventually found widespread success as a motivational author, writing several books on how to achieve success and practically creating the self-help genre.

Aim High,
ACHIEVE MORE

The *Roadmap* to *Fulfillment*

NAPOLEON HILL

RUPA

Published by
Rupa Publications India Pvt. Ltd 2024
7/16, Ansari Road, Daryaganj
New Delhi 110002

Sales centres:
Bengaluru Chennai
Hyderabad Jaipur Kathmandu
Kolkata Mumbai Prayagraj

Edition copyright © Rupa Publications India Pvt. Ltd 2024

All rights reserved.
No part of this publication may be reproduced, transmitted,
or stored in a retrieval system, in any form or by any means, electronic,
mechanical, photocopying, recording or otherwise, without the prior
permission of the publisher.

P-ISBN: 978-93-5702-902-5
E-ISBN: 978-93-5702-976-6

First impression 2024

10 9 8 7 6 5 4 3 2 1

Printed in India

This book is sold subject to the condition that it shall not, by way of
trade or otherwise, be lent, resold, hired out, or otherwise circulated,
without the publisher's prior consent, in any form of binding or
cover other than that in which it is published.

CONTENTS

1. It Is up to You to Live the Life the Creator Gave You   7
2. Will You Dare to Explore the Powers of Your Mind?   28
3. A Definite Chief Aim   45
4. Concentration   52
5. Imagination   71
6. Failure   87
7. You've Got a Problem? That's Good!   90
8. How to Outwit the Ghosts of Fear   96
9. The Mastery of Poverty   127
10. The Habit of Saving   134
11. The 17 Principles of Success   148

1

IT IS UP TO YOU TO LIVE THE LIFE THE CREATOR GAVE YOU

You have a great potential for success, but first you must know your own mind and live your own life—then you will find and enjoy that mighty potential. Become acquainted with your inner self and you can win what you want within a time limit of your own choosing. Certain special techniques help you win the goals of your dearest dreams, and every one of these techniques is easily within your power.

Somewhere along the path of life, every successful man finds out how to live his own life as he wishes to live it.

The younger you are when you discover this mighty power, the more likely you are to live successfully and happily. Yet even in later years, many make the great change—from letting others make them what they are, to making sure that they make their lives to their own liking.

The Creator gave man the prerogative of power over his own mind. It must have been the Creator's purpose to encourage man to live his own life, think his own thoughts, find his own goals and achieve them. Simply by exercising this profound prerogative you can bring abundance into your life, and with it know the greatest wealth of all, peace of mind, without which there can be no real happiness.

You live in a world filled with outside influences which impinge upon you. You are influenced by other people's acts and wishes, by law and custom, by your duties and your responsibilities. Everything you do has some effect upon others, as do their actions upon you. And yet you must find out how to live your own life, use your own mind, go on toward the dream you wish to make real and solid. 'Know thyself,' said the ancient Greek philosophers, and this remains key advice for the man who would be in all ways wealthy. Without knowing yourself and being yourself, you cannot truly use the one Great Secret which gives you power to mold your future and make life carry you the way you want to go.

Let us then take off on our trip to Happy Valley!

Do not think of me as a back-seat driver. Rather, you are at the wheel and I merely call your attention to a trustworthy road map whereon the main highway is marked beyond question. On your journey to riches and peace of mind, the road grows smoother and straighter as you travel.

Never believe you don't have what it takes. Probably you are reading under an electric light. You know that Thomas A. Edison gave the first practical electric light to the world. But did you know that Edison was thrown out of school in the early grades after his teacher decided he had an 'addled' mind and could not take schooling?

This then was the impact of another person's opinion upon Thomas Edison—to let him know with the voice of authority that he didn't have what it takes to absorb even a primary education! Where would he have been if he had allowed this directive to take charge of his thinking?

Fortunately for him and fortunately for the world, Edison

decided to live his own life. Through early adversity, Edison discovered something he might never have learned through formal schooling. He learned, first, that he had a mind he could control and direct toward any desired end. Then he learned he could use the technical training of other men and successfully direct scientific research even though he himself never had been schooled in any of the sciences. When he took full possession of that 'addled' mind it produced not only the incandescent lamp but also one great discovery after another.

A boy finds a friend and finds himself. I too was nearly doomed by a false label of unworthiness. I was then nine years old. My mother had died a year before, and I lived with relatives. To them and to my own father I was a problem child who never would accomplish anything save, perhaps, what a life of crime can accomplish.

I was doing my best to live up to my reputation as the successor of Jesse James. I even had a six-shooter which I had learned to handle like an expert. Then a certain woman came upon the scene and she changed my life. That woman was my stepmother.

Long before she arrived, I had been thoroughly conditioned by my relatives to hate her. I found this very easy to do. She arrived, and my father brought her to our house where the relatives had gathered to meet her. He introduced her all around. At length he found me, where I stood in a corner doing my very best to look tough.

'And here,' said my father, 'is your stepson, Napoleon, beyond doubt the meanest boy in Wise County. We don't expect much good from him. I wouldn't be surprised if he starts throwing rocks at you by tomorrow morning.'

At that moment, I believe my life hung in the balance.

It was a wise and wonderful woman who placed her hand

under my stubborn chin and raised my head so that she could look me squarely in the eyes. She said only a few words, but they lifted me onto an entirely new level.

Turning to my father, my stepmother said, 'You are wrong about this boy. He is not the meanest boy in Wise County or anywhere else. He is a very alert and intelligent boy, and all he needs is some worthy objective toward which to direct his very good mind.'

That was the first time in my life that anyone had said anything good about me. I straightened up, threw out my chest and grinned. Then and there I sensed that 'that woman' who had come to take my mother's place—as my relatives referred to her—was one of those rare people who can help others find the best that is in them.

That was the end of my six-shooter days. Increasingly finding myself as I grew older, I discovered my talent for writing. My stepmother helped me master the typewriter. With the aid of the typewriter, I became a writer for newspapers. Through that experience I qualified to interview successful men, and thus I came to sit down with Andrew Carnegie. Out of that interview—which ran on through the better part of three days and nights—came my commitment to search out the secret of successful achievement, not merely as a matter of words, but as a pattern of definite action in the lives of men who have achieved great wealth. Out of this grew the organization of the Science of Personal Achievement which has reverberated around the world, bringing prosperity and peace of mind to millions of men and women.

Great artists also live their own lives, or they could not be great. One of the great opera stars of all time, Madame Schumann-Heink, as a young girl went to a music teacher to have her voice tested. He listened a few minutes, then said brusquely, 'That's enough! Go back to your sewing machine. You may become a first-class seamstress. A singer, no!'

Remember, that was the voice of authority speaking. The girl could have been forgiven for deciding then and there that she would never sing again. Yet she had and kept possession of her own mind. She became all the more determined that she would learn to sing and to sing well. This she did, and the world became richer. So it has been with many another case in which great personal talent might have been lost forever if the possessor of that talent had not felt it even when the 'experts' said it was not there.

Adversity? It's a tonic, not a stumbling block! Every adversity carries the seed of an equal or greater benefit. Very few march straight to success without going through periods of temporary failure and discouragement. Yet when you are in possession of your inner self there is no such thing as a knockout blow. You may be knocked down, but you can bounce right back. You may detour on rough roads, but you always can find your way back to the paved highway.

You may think this applies only to simple matters. Think, then, of the infinitely complex matter of winning the independence of a colonial territory—and not only that, but of focusing the many scattered influences which make sure you become the country's first President.

In 1910, I became the personal counsellor of Manuel L. Quezon. I not only counselled him politically but, perhaps more importantly, I taught him the Science of Personal Achievement which then was quite new.

Señor Quezon was the first President of the Philippine Islands when they gained their freedom. In 1910, however, that time was far in the future. The goal of freeing his people possessed Quezon's mind, and he saw himself as the first

President of the new nation. I assured him he could realize both ambitions, yet we knew that such great events do not come to pass overnight.

FIND YOUR GOAL

There is a well-recognized power in setting up a definite goal. Few, however, realize the power of setting a realistic time limit in which one intends to attain that goal. After having counselled Senor Quezon for some years, I induced him to set a definite time limit for freeing the Philippines and becoming the new nation's leader. I also prepared an affirmation which he repeated to himself daily. It closed with a statement of this nature, 'I will allow no person's opinion, no influence to enter my mind which does not harmonize with my purpose.' Both the time limit and the affirmation were of great help to Quezon in knowing his own mind and keeping his own direction in the face of the enormous difficulties which beset him.

Twenty-four years and six months from the day Quezon began to use the Science of Personal Achievement, he became the first President of the free Philippine Islands.

Coincidence? Coincidence despite a world war which intervened and many other factors which were not foreseeable? I do not think it was a coincidence, for I have seen this principle of Personal Achievement work for so many people in so many different situations that coincidence must be ruled out.

We shall touch upon the principle again. Right now I shall tell you about just one man, presently doing business in Chicago, who has used it with notable success.

W. Clement Stone was in high school when he discovered his own goals, his own direction in which the powers of his own mind would take him. Soon he was selling insurance at such a rate that he made more money than his teachers. Today his fortune is estimated at more than $160 million and it is increasing rapidly.

In 1939, however, he faced disaster. At that time, he was the head of an agency, representing a big casualty company, which sold a special accident and health policy. One day the parent company 'pulled the string' and terminated his contract with two weeks' notice.

Mr Stone did not have large reserves. It was imperative to keep that contract going. He spent forty-five minutes in refreshing his contact with his inner self; then he decided that within those critical two weeks he would persuade the casualty company it was against their own best interest to terminate his contract. The company had very cogent reasons for ending the contract. Nevertheless, they did change their minds as he wished them to and Stone kept on marching toward his fortune.

He then decided that by 1956 he would own his own big health and accident insurance company. By 1956 he did.

He decided that by 1956 he would have $10 million dollars of his own. He did.

I heard recently that Mr Stone has set up a lifetime goal of $600 million. I do not know his deadline date, but I have no doubt that on or before that date he will have the stated sum; and further, that he will use a good part of it as he always has used his money—to benefit mankind. The concept of $600 million may frighten a man who thinks small, but a man who knows the secrets of Personal Achievement merely says: why not?

A little while ago I made a survey for the purpose of learning who were the ten men who had made the most outstanding application of the Science of Personal Achievement in the United States.

W. Clement Stone was third from the top of the list. The other two were Andrew Carnegie, the sponsor of my twenty years of research, and Thomas Alva Edison, the greatest inventor of all time.

I met Mr Stone for the first time in 1953. It was then that I began to unravel the dramatic story of his rise to fame and fortune, starting in business for himself with only one hundred dollars in cash and a copy of my most popular book, *Think and Grow Rich*. I was so intrigued by the effective application Stone had made of my success philosophy that I accepted his offer to help him take the Science of Personal Achievement to his entire insurance personnel.

The task covered ten years during which I devoted all of my time to helping Mr Stone indoctrinate his entire organization with my success philosophy. It was a tremendous job but it paid off in terms which proved conclusively that my twenty years of research under the direction of Andrew Carnegie had uncovered a miraculous formula for helping people to get from where they were to where they wished to be in life.

When I first began my association with Mr Stone, many of his top executives frowned upon the alliance as being a waste of time. They had never heard of a success philosophy based upon what five hundred outstanding men had learned from a lifetime of experience through the trial-and-error method and they were naturally suspicious of it.

Five years later these same executives met with Mr Stone and myself in a business conference. To my great surprise Mr Stone arose and addressed himself to the group. 'Gentlemen,' said he, 'the Combined Insurance Company of America is now performing miracles.' Then a long pause, after which he said, 'The company was performing no miracles before Napoleon Hill came here.'

When I began my association with Mr Stone the annual premium income from policy holders was around $24 million, and Mr Stone's personal fortune was estimated to be around $3 million. When the association was discontinued by mutual consent ten years later, the annual premium income of the company was around $84 million and Mr Stone's personal fortune was estimated to be more than $160 million.

'How much did I get from the association?' you may wish to ask. The cash I received was negligible in comparison with that which Mr Stone received, but I was not working for monetary reward; I was after something far greater than that which could have been gained by any amount of money, for I had proved during those ten years of association with Mr Stone that the Science of Personal Achievement could perform miracles for those who embraced it and made intelligent application of it.

More important still, I had laid the foundation for the Napoleon Hill Academy, which is now organizing and conducting franchise schools for the teaching of the Science of Personal Achievement throughout the United States and eventually will reach throughout the free world. The far-flung significance of these schools may be brought into understandable focus by the fact that the Science of Personal Achievement has turned out to be a perfect antidote for communism; something I had not anticipated when I began the organization of the philosophy in 1908. Which reminds me that, truly, 'man proposes but God disposes.'

SUCCESS CONSCIOUSNESS

It may well be that the Science of Personal Achievement will become a strong factor in neutralizing the cancerous evil known as communism, which now threatens the liberty of all mankind.

The Science of Personal Achievement is already under option to a group of men who are having it translated into Spanish for the purpose of taking it to the people of all Spanish-speaking countries, starting with our Latin-American friends of the South. I plan eventually to have the philosophy translated into all the major languages of the world.

So, who is wise enough to say what I got from my ten years of association with W. Clement Stone, or wise enough to understand the hand of fate which brought the two of us together?

The dramatic story of Arnold Reed. Arnold Reed is another insurance executive whose life story and its relation to the Science of Personal Achievement parallels that of W. Clement Stone. In many respects his story, as it related to the success philosophy, is more dramatic than the Stone story.

Mr Reed was a top-ranking life insurance salesman, with a record of sales production seldom equalled by anyone in this field. Mr Reed's sales started at around one million dollars annually and pyramided upward far beyond this amount. He was associated with an insurance company headed by a man whom he regarded as his personal friend.

Unfortunately (or was it?) Arnold had not read carefully the fine print of his contract with the company, for he learned later that it contained a clause which deprived him of his renewal premium commissions, the one factor in the insurance salesman's work which gives him his greatest incentive to do a good job.

This discovery shocked Arnold so severely that he went home and went to bed, refusing to eat or to communicate with his friends. Doctors were called in to diagnose his ailment but not one of them could find anything wrong with him physically. It was not his body that was sick, it was his soul, for the shock he had experienced through the perfidy of his friend had cut the line of communication between him and the source of inspiration which had made him a great life insurance salesman; that source which alone can make men truly great!

Slowly but surely Arnold Reed was dying.

His ailment was one that no doctor could cure. The doctors who had attended him knew this and frankly admitted they could offer no hope. Then a miracle happened. A friend of Arnold's, who had long been a student of my success philosophy, visited Arnold and presented him with *Think and Grow Rich*. 'Here is a book,' he told Arnold, 'which has worked wonders for me and I want you to read it.'

Arnold took the book, threw it on the bed beside him and turned away without comment. Hours later he picked up the book, opened it and, lo! something in it caught his eye and he read it through. Then he read it again, and again, and on the third time around he felt the surge of a power which he readily recognized as one which could bring him out of the dungeon of despair into which he had fallen.

He got out of bed and began to write letters to his friends who knew of his record as a life insurance salesman, offering them an opportunity to join with him in organizing a life insurance company under the name of Great Commonwealth Life Insurance Company.

The friends responded quickly and generously. The amount of money needed was oversubscribed and much of it had to be returned to the senders. All of this took place at about the time I was beginning my alliance with W. Clement Stone.

Now, some twelve years later, the Great Commonwealth Life Insurance Company is one of the most successful in its field, with a gross premium income of over $9 million in 1966, and rapidly increasing toward the new goal which Arnold Reed has set at a billion dollars annually.

The company is operating in a major portion of the United States and it has a sales organization of over four hundred dedicated men and women who have tuned in and drawn upon that mysterious power that brought Arnold Reed out of the shadows of death; and they are doing a job that is without parallel in the insurance industry.

The Great Commonwealth Life Insurance Company conducts schools in many parts of the country in which new recruits to its sales force are trained. The first thing each trainee receives is a copy of *Think and Grow Rich* and a briefing on what this book has done for Arnold Reed and the company.

The last time I spoke to the sales organization of the Great Commonwealth Life Insurance Company, Arnold Reed marched onto the platform holding me by the arm. He held up a copy of *Think and Grow Rich* as he said, 'My friends, if it had not been for this book and my dear friend here on my left, there would have been no Great Commonwealth Life Insurance Company and I would now be six feet under the ground.'

It was the shortest and the most dramatic introduction I had ever experienced, and it filled me so deeply with emotion that I could hardly begin my speech.

Arnold Reed is a truly great leader of men, as evidenced by the phenomenal record he has established with Great Commonwealth. The main secret of his leadership is his belief in what he is doing and his sincerity in his relationship with his associates, two qualities without which no man may become a great leader at any level of life.

A success-conscious mind functions rapidly and effectively. In my hundreds of interviews with men who had made fortunes, I noticed how well their minds were focussed on success. Some of these men were well educated. Some, for example Henry Ford, were notably uninformed in some areas of 'school learning'. It never was the formal education or the lack of it which gave these men the power to use their minds with such drive and effect, nor was it unusual intelligence. What was it, then, which impelled their minds to seize upon great goals, then winnow all the circumstances of life and make use of what could help them achieve their ambitions? It was *success consciousness*.

First you must know your own mind; then you find success consciousness. When Henry Ford mastered the art of making a good, inexpensive automobile, he still went on using his success consciousness. He had to make sure his cars were well distributed and their sale pushed in every part of the country. For this he needed capital. The bankers had capital to lend, but he did not want outside financial interests to take hold of his company.

Ford's truly efficient mind showed him the way to get the capital he needed even while he built up his distributing organization. First, he allotted his entire output of automobiles only to distributors who held the Ford franchise. Then he made it clear that each distributor must accept a fixed quota of cars, advancing in cash a percentage of the purchase price before the cars were delivered.

This plan made every distributor practically a partner in the Ford business, yet it did not affect Mr Ford's control of the business. Again, without affecting his control, it provided him with the necessary operating capital. Moreover, it provided his dealers with a very definite incentive toward finding a buyer for every car—actually the same incentive they would have had if they had been operating their own independent businesses.

I have heard it said that this plan worked a hardship on some of the Ford distributors. Having known some dealers since before the Model T car, however, and having looked at today's record, I can say that most Ford dealers are noteworthy for their success.

Two bicycle mechanics, Orville and Wilbur Wright, gave the world its first successful airplane. What kept their minds clicking, caused them first to build the world's first wind tunnel, caused them to find a secret of wingtip control which nobody else had thought of? What caused them to surmount limitations of material and of power which still make that first flight look 'impossible'? First, they took control of their own minds and their own lives; then they were guided by the success consciousness which always follows.

Is today's world different? Only in some details. Take such a device as a memory core, a tiny magnetic gadget which operates by the thousands in many modern computers. The Wright brothers did not know of such things, nor did Henry Ford or Andrew Carnegie or Thomas Edison. A young man named Merlyn Mickelson, in 1955, looked at the rapidly dawning computer age and saw what every age offers—a need and a way to fill it. He started to manufacture memory cores in his basement. His first investment in tools and supplies came to $7.21. His first employees were friends and neighbouring housewives who 'pitched in'. Today, not yet forty, Mr Mickelson still makes memory cores. He is President and 75 per cent owner of a $16-million-year company, and the company stock he holds is worth about $47 million.

THE SPIRITUAL FORCE

Can success consciousness be instilled into a mind already filled with a record of failure? When you come to know your own mind and live your own life, you can wipe out a record of failure just as surely as you can erase the message on a tape recorder, leaving a wonderfully receptive tape—or mind—to receive new and better impressions.

Some people have been able to do this for themselves. Others need help. I well remember a man I helped to find himself. As you will see, I got him started and once he knew where he was going, he did the rest.

This was a dead-broke man just out of the Army. I believe he used the Army as a refuge, but eventually he was back in civilian clothes, looking for a job. The mere mention of 'hard times' seemed to be enough to flatten him. He was shabby. He was hungry. He was willing to settle for crumbs if only he could get them.

He came to see me about finding work. At the outset he announced, 'All I want is a place to sleep and enough to eat.'

A place to sleep and enough to eat—in a world that throbs with riches!

Something prompted me to ask, 'Why settle for a meal ticket? How would you like to become a millionaire?'

He looked at me with glassy eyes, swaying, 'Please don't joke with me.'

'I assure you I'm serious. Every man has some kind of assets, and every man can turn his assets into a million dollars or many millions if he uses them correctly.'

He sighed. 'What do you mean by assets? I have a nickel in my pocket.'

'Bring your mind around to the positive side,' I said, 'and

you have the most important asset you'll ever have. We'll work on that. Now let's take inventory of your skills. Sit down, we'll talk better. What did you do in the Army?'

He had been a cook. Before going into the Army he had been a Fuller Brush salesman. He was a good cook, I discovered, but obviously he had not been a good salesman. Still, he knew something about selling and in talking to him, I discovered he still wanted to sell. At the outset, however, he had no belief he ever could become a good salesman. The memory of past failures inhibited him and I had to help him break those self-inflicted mental blocks and see, not what he had been, but what he could be.

We talked for some time and meanwhile my own mind was busily at work. My mind was not weakened by hunger and hopelessness. There had been a time when my mind had known as much despair as did his; but now I was filled with success consciousness.

Questing about, my uninhibited mind remembered that special new kinds of cookware were now being developed. A new kind of cookware of great benefit to the housewife—a man who could think about cooking and even demonstrate—a man who could be made into a good salesman—and there we had the winning combination.

'Suppose you represented a company that makes a new kind of aluminium cookware,' I said. 'This cookware offers many advantages. It should be seen in action; then it will practically sell itself. Any housewife, for a small consideration say, some free pots or pans for her own use—should be glad to invite her neighbours in for a home-cooked dinner. You cook that dinner with the special cookware, and after dinner you take orders for complete, matched sets. If twenty ladies are present, I'm sure you could induce half of them to purchase. Some of these would be eager to run similar dinner parties in their own homes. The business would become self-perpetuating.'

'Sounds okay,' my young soldier friend replied. 'But where am I going to sleep meanwhile? And where am I going to eat? And where am I going to get a few clean shirts and a new suit? Not to mention the question of where I am going to get some money or credit to get started on?'

Such questions are typical of the mind which does not yet know itself, and so sums up all the obstacles rather than looking directly at the goal.

'Get yourself into the right frame of mind,' I said, 'and you will either find what you need or find a way to do without and still achieve your goal. When your mind can truly picture a desired goal, and feel success consciousness driving it toward that goal, you can win that goal. Let us put aside all other matters and investigate your state of mind.'

Actually, the young man was very close to having the desired positive state of mind. I waited till I was sure he had it, however. Then I said he was a good risk, and I gave him the use of our guest room, and his meals. I let him use my charge account at Marshall Field's so that he could be well dressed. I guaranteed his note for his first outfit of cookware.

During his first week he cleared nearly one hundred dollars in profit. The second week he doubled that amount. In a little while he began to train other men and women, whom he managed. Most of all, he instilled in them the success consciousness which now had full hold of his mind, and as they prospered, so did he.

At the end of four years, the young man who had been so hungry and broken-spirited, so very far from being a millionaire, was worth more than four million dollars. Moreover, his newly keen and efficient mind had perfected a home-demonstration selling plan which now nets millions of dollars annually to a large corps of salespeople.

When the bells of heaven ring with joy. When a man finds his own mind and fills it with successful consciousness, or when another man helps him do so, I fancy that the bells of heaven ring with joy. Here is one more soul who has broken the chains forged by his fearful imagination.

Now you can see why I chose to begin this book by revealing what it means to take possession of your own mind, live your own life, find your real self that has no limitations. When you do this, you have an asset worth whatever value you choose to make it worth.

Think again of what is involved in creating an independent nation. Think of ancient India with its teeming millions, under British rule for generation after generation. Think of the Mahatma Gandhi, a man who had no money, controlled no army, did not own a house, did not even own a pair of pants. Yet he had an asset which was greater than all the might of the British Empire—the capacity to take possession of his own mind and direct it toward purposes of his own choosing. He chose to free India, and he lived to see the achievement of his purpose.

Thanks to the influence of Mahatma Gandhi, my Science of Personal Achievement now has many millions of followers in India. Whether your goal is money, the well-being of others or a combination of these—as well it may be—know that there is nothing beyond the power of a mind that knows itself and believes in its own capabilities.

The spiritual defenses within the castle of your mind. I have purposely used the word 'defenses' in order to call your attention to its varying meanings. A mind that is 'on the defensive' is not an open mind. It is more likely to be a frightened mind, full of excuses and evasions and hardly capable of lifting its possessor's eyes to the far horizons of accomplishment. In speaking of spiritual defenses, then, I speak of nothing that is negative: rather I speak of certain areas within which one may withdraw and thus become more completely one's *self.*

Every successful person I have known has surrounded himself with these spiritual defenses in one way or another. I adopted the system, and have found it invaluable. Here is how it works.

Consider your mind to be laid out in the pattern of some medieval castles. At the centre there is a tower, or 'keep', which is as impregnable as it can be made. Going outward from the keep you would come to a wall not so formidable; and again going outward you would come to another wall which serves as the first line of defense.

A person approaching the castle first would have to pass the outer wall. This wall of spiritual defense in your mind need not be very high. Anyone who has a legitimate excuse for entering your mind with his ideas can climb this wall. If he does not have a legitimate excuse, however, the wall discourages him. When you set up such a wall, others come to know it is there and you give yourself a valuable protection.

A person who passes the first line of defense now confronts the second line which you may set up on certain occasions and not on others. When your mind sets up this wall, nobody may climb it unless that person has something strongly in common with you, or something importantly beneficial to share with you at that moment.

The inmost castle of protection is the most important of all. It is small, barely big enough to surround you, but when your mind retreats within that keep it is removed from every outside influence. With me, only the Creator can penetrate my inmost spiritual castle. Find yours and you find a source of great strength. Here is where you can find your inmost thoughts, undisturbed by outside influences; and until you find this castle you never can know them. Here is where you can search all the values of a problem and find a solution which otherwise you might not see. Here, especially, is where your fully possessed mind reveals what can be done—and when you come out of your retreat you know that it will be done and that you will do it.

At first you may find it necessary to retreat physically from the world into a quiet room or perhaps to some place distant from your business and from people who know you. This often is a good idea even when you have practice in finding the most inmost privacy of your mind, because there are many physical circumstances which break into thought.

When you have several times retreated to your thick-walled keep, however, you will find you can enter it for a few seconds even in the midst of others who are talking all around you. I have seen many successful men do this, and thus illustrate some of the power to which they owe their success. It is a great renewer of the spirit, a kind of recharge of ability and self-confidence and abiding faith.

All that I have to say in this book is keyed to one Supreme Secret.

This Secret has been strongly sketched in throughout this chapter. You have seen it, and already it is beginning to penetrate your subconscious mind—which never forgets.

POINTS TO REMEMBER

1. Fear has no place in a well-lived life.
2. Peace of mind, the greatest of the riches and how to find it.
3. Find the power to turn what the human mind believes into what the human mind achieves.

2

WILL YOU DARE TO EXPLORE THE POWERS OF YOUR MIND?

"You are a mind with a body!"

Because you are a mind, *you* possess mystical powers—powers known and unknown. Dare to explore the powers of your mind! Why explore them?

When you make the discoveries that are awaiting you, they can bring you: (1) physical, mental and moral health, happiness and wealth; (2) success in your chosen field of endeavour; and even (3) a means to affect, use, control or harmonize with powers known and unknown.

And dare to investigate all non-physical forces lying outside the realm of known physical processes—forces which you can use when you learn how to apply them. And this will not be so difficult for you—no more difficult than turning on a television set for the first time.

For a little child can tune into his favourite television program. Now, when he does, he neither knows the construction of the broadcasting station or his receiving set, nor the technology involved. But that's all right. For all the child needs to know is how to turn the right knob or push the right button.

You will see in this chapter how you can turn the right knob or push the right button to get what you want from the most effective electrical machine ever conceived. Although this particular machine is the sublime handiwork of Divine Power—you own it. How is it made? Well, among other things, it is comprised of over 80 trillion electrical cells. Naturally, it has many component parts. And each part is in itself an electrical mechanism.

And one part is an electrical marvel. Yet it weighs only fifty ounces. Its mechanism consists of over 10 billion cells which generate, receive, record and transmit energy.

What is this wonderful machine that you own? Your body. You are and will be the same *you* even though you lose an arm, an eye or other parts of your body.

And the electrical marvel? *Your brain and your nervous system. It is the mechanism through which your body is controlled and through which your mind functions.*

And your mind: it, too, has parts. One is known as the conscious, and the other the subconscious. They synchronize. They work together. Scientists have learned a great deal about the conscious mind. Yet it has been less than a hundred years since we began to explore the vast unknown territory of the subconscious—even though primitive man has deliberately used the mystical powers of the subconscious from the beginning of man's history, and even today the Aborigines of Australia and other primitive peoples do so to a very great extent.

Let's start exploring now!

Day by day in every way I'm getting richer and richer! Let's begin by accompanying Bill McCall of Sydney, Australia on a journey from failure and defeat to success and achievement.

It was at the age of 19 that Bill started a business of his own—hides and skins. He failed. At the age of 21 he ran for Federal Congress. And again he failed. Now it seems that instead of crushing him, these and other defeats motivated this young Australian to develop inspirational dissatisfaction.

So he began searching for rules of success.

You see, Bill McCall wanted to become rich, and he thought he could find rules for acquiring wealth in inspirational books. Therefore, while checking the inspirational book section of the library, Bill became intrigued by the title *Think and Grow Rich*. He borrowed the book and began to read. He read it once, and then he read it again. And even though he read it the third time, Bill McCall was unable to understand exactly how he could apply the principles whereby some of the richest men in the world acquired their wealth. He told us:

'I was reading *Think and Grow Rich* for the fourth time while walking leisurely along a business street in Sydney. And then it happened! It happened suddenly. I stopped in front of a meat market window and glanced up. And in that very fraction of a second I had a flash of inspiration.' He smiled as he continued:

'I exclaimed aloud, "That's it! I've got it!" I was startled at my emotional outburst. So was a lady who was passing by. She stopped and looked at me in amazement. I hurried home with my new discovery.' He continued seriously:

'You see, I was reading Chapter Four entitled *Autosuggestion*. The subheading was *The Medium for Influencing the Subconscious Mind*.

'Now I remember that when I was a boy my father read aloud from Emile Coué's little book *Self-Mastery Through Conscious Autosuggestion*.' He then looked at me and said:

'It was you who pointed out in your book that if Emile Coué was successful in helping individuals avoid sickness and in bringing the sick back to good health, through conscious autosuggestion, autosuggestion could also be used to acquire riches or anything else one might desire. "Get rich through autosuggestion": that was my great discovery. It was a new concept to me.' McCall then described the principles. It almost seemed as if he had memorized them from the book itself.

'You know: conscious autosuggestion is the agency of control through which an individual may voluntarily feed his subconscious mind on thoughts of a creative nature, or, by neglect, permit thoughts of a destructive nature to find their way into the rich garden of his mind.

'When you read aloud twice daily the written statement of your desire for money with emotion and concentrated attention, and you see and feel yourself already in possession of the money, you communicate the object of your desire directly to your subconscious mind. Through repetition of this procedure, you voluntarily create thought habits which are favourable to your efforts to transmute desire into its monetary equivalent.

'Let me say again: it is most important that when you read aloud the statement of your desire through which you are endeavouring to develop a money consciousness, you read with emotion and strong feeling.

'Your ability to use the principles of autosuggestion will depend very largely upon your capacity to concentrate upon a given desire until that desire becomes a burning desire.

'When I arrived home, out of breath for running, I immediately sat down at the dining room table and wrote, "My definite major aim is to be a millionaire by 1960."' Still looking at me, he continued, 'You mentioned that a person should be specific as to the amount of money he wants and set a date. I did.'

Now, the man to whom we were talking was not the young Bill McCall who failed at the age of 19. He became known as the Honourable William V. McCall, the youngest man ever to become a member of the Australian Parliament; as the former chairman of the board of directors of the CocaCola subsidiary in Sydney; and as the director of 22 family-owned corporations. And as to riches—he became a millionaire, and quite as rich as some of the men he had read about in the book from which he got the inspiration *to explore the power of his subconscious mind with self-suggestion.* (Incidentally, he became a millionaire four years ahead of schedule!)

Day by day in every way I am getting better and better! *You will note we use the term 'self-suggestion' as being synonymous with the term 'conscious autosuggestion' used by Emile Coué.*

McCall remembered that when he was a boy his father had benefited from a great discovery found in a book of his day—a discovery that every man, woman and child can effectively employ when he finds it for himself. Like Bill McCall and his father, you too can properly employ the power of conscious autosuggestion.

CONSCIOUS SUGGESTION

Now conscious autosuggestion was revealed to Emile Coué because he dared to explore the powers of his own mind and the minds of others. Before he made his great discovery, he used hypnosis to cure the physical illnesses of his patients. But after making his great discovery, which was in reality based on a simple natural law, he abandoned the use of hypnosis.

And how did he find and recognize this natural law?

Emile Coué's great discovery was made when he found the answer to some questions he asked himself. They were:

Question No. 1: Is it the suggestion of the doctor, or is it the

suggestion in the mind of the patient, that effects a cure?
Answer: Coué proved conclusively that it was the mind of the patient that subconsciously or consciously made the suggestion to which his own mind and body reacted. Without either (unconscious) autosuggestion or conscious autosuggestion, external suggestions are not effective.

Question No. 2: If the suggestion of the doctor stimulates internal suggestion of the patient, why can't the patient use healthful, positive suggestions on himself? And why can't he refrain from harmful negative suggestions?
Answer: The answer to his second question came quickly: anyone, even a child, can be taught to develop a positive mental attitude. The method is to repeat positive affirmations such as: *day by day, in every way, through the grace of God, I am getting better and better.*

Throughout *Success Through a Positive Mental Attitude*, you will see many self-motivators which you can use for your own self-suggestion. And if by now you don't know how to use self-suggestion, you will before you complete this book.

When death's door is about to open. There are over 450,000 children born out of wedlock in the United States each year, and over a million and a half teen-agers enter penal institutions for car thefts and other crimes. These personal tragedies could in many instances be avoided if: (a) the parents learned how to employ suggestion properly, and (b) if their sons and daughters were taught how effectively to use spiritual self-suggestion. Through the proper use of suggestion, these young people could be motivated to develop inviolable moral standards through their own conscious autosuggestion. And they would know how to neutralize or repel the undesirable suggestions of their associates in an intelligent manner.

Of course, every individual responds to (unconscious) autosuggestion throughout his life more often than he does to conscious autosuggestion. In such instances he responds to habit and the inner urge of the subconscious. When a man with PMA is faced with a serious personal problem, self-motivators flash from the subconscious to the conscious to aid him. This is especially true in times of emergency—especially when death's door is about to be opened. Such was the case with Ralph Weppner of Toowoomba, Queensland, Australia, one of our PMA Science of Success course students.

It was 1:30 in the morning. In a small hospital bedroom two nursing sisters were keeping vigil beside Ralph's body. At 4:30 the afternoon before an emergency call had been made to his family to rush to the hospital. When they arrived at his bedside, Ralph was in a state of coma as the result of a severe heart attack. The family was now out in the corridor, each one worrying or praying in his own special way.

In the dimly lit bedroom two nursing sisters worked anxiously—one on each wrist—trying to feel a pulse beat. Because Ralph had not come out of the coma during this entire six-hour period and the doctor had done all that he felt he could, the doctor had left the room. He had gone to visit one of his other hospital patients who was also in a critical condition.

Ralph couldn't move, talk or feel anything. Yet he could hear the voices of the sisters. He could think quite clearly during portions of this period. He heard one sister excitedly state:

'He's not breathing! Can you pick up a beat?'

The answer was, 'No.'

Again and again he heard the question and answer, 'Can you now pick up a beat?' 'No.'

'I'm all right,' he thought, 'but I must tell them. Somehow

I must tell them.'

At the same time he was amused at the sisters for being fooled like that. He kept thinking, 'I'm quite all right. I'm not going to die. But how—how—can I tell them?'

And then he remembered the self-motivator he had learned: You can do it if you believe you can!

He tried to open his eyes, but it seemed the more he tried, the more he failed. His eyelids wouldn't respond to the command of his will. He tried to move his arm, his leg, his head—but he couldn't feel any reaction at all. In fact, he didn't feel a thing. Again and again he tried to open his eyes, until at last he heard the words, 'I saw one eyelid flicker—he's still there.'

'I felt no fear,' Ralph says, 'and still thought how amusing it was. Periodically one sister called to me, "Are you there, Mr Weppner? Are you there?" To which I would try to respond by moving my eyelid to tell them that I was all right—I was still there.'

This went on for a considerable time until through constant effort Ralph was at last able to open one, then both eyes. It was then that his doctor returned. With wonderful skill and persistence the doctor and nurses brought him back to life.

Hidden persuaders. But it was the autosuggestion: you can do it if you believe you can—that he had memorized from the PMA Science of Success course—that helped to rescue him when he was at death's door.

THE HIDDEN FORCES

Now the books we read and the thoughts we think affect our subconscious minds. But there are also unseen forces that likewise have powerful effects even though they are subliminal—below the realm of consciousness.

These unseen forces can be from known physical causes or from unknown sources. Before discussing the unknown, let's illustrate with an example that is now common knowledge since the publishing of *Hidden Persuaders* by Vance Packard. The story first appeared in American newspapers and later was picked up in magazines. Let's consider a report that appeared in a leading national magazine on the subject of subliminal advertising. The report tells of an experiment conducted in a New Jersey movie theatre, in which advertising messages were flashed on the screen so fast that the viewers were not consciously aware of them.

During a period of six weeks, more than forty thousand persons unknowingly became subjects of this test, while attending the theatre. Flashed on the screen by a special process that made them invisible to the naked eye were two advertising messages concerning products that were available in the theatre lobby. At the end of the six weeks, results were tabulated: sales of one of the products had soared over 50 per cent, while sales of the other product rose almost 20 per cent.

The inventor of the process explained that, although the messages were invisible, they still had taken effect on many in the audience because of the ability of the subconscious mind to absorb impressions that are too fleeting to be registered consciously.

When this story appeared in the press, the public was horrified 'by this attempt to channel our thinking habits, our purchasing decisions and our thought processes' by the use of subliminal suggestion. People were afraid. They feared brainwashing in its most subtle form. Yet it is amazing to us that someone didn't take the PMA approach. Subliminal suggestion can be employed for desirable objectives, too. Everyone knows that power can be used for evil or for good, depending upon how it is directed.

Now that the experiment has proved its purpose, it doesn't take much imagination to see what the beneficial results to the viewers would be should the following self-motivators be flashed on a movie screen:

God is always a good God!

Day by day, in every way, through the grace of God, you are getting better and better!

Have the courage to face the truth!

What the mind of man can conceive and believe, the mind of man can achieve with PMA!

Every adversity has the seed of an equivalent or greater benefit for those who have a positive mental attitude!

You can do it if you believe you can!

This would be a PMA approach, provided, of course, the consent of the audience was obtained in advance.

Another illustration of a known physical force affecting the subconscious mind can be shown by the effect of radar on navigators.

Why did the SS Andrea Doria and the SS Valchem sink? When the Andrea Doria, captained by Pierre Clamai, and the Stockholm, under Captain H. O. Nordenson, collided approximately 50 miles off Nantucket Island, 50 persons died.

The Andrea Doria was sighted by the radar operator of the Stockholm when they were 10 miles apart.

The Grace Line luxury liner, the Santa Rosa under Captain Frank S. Siwik, collided with the tanker Valchem on March 26, 1959, 22 miles off the New Jersey coast. Four crewmen were killed. Second Mate Walter Wells, the radar operator on the Santa Rosa, claimed he had made two plottings of the tanker Valchem's course.

No satisfactory explanation of the true cause of these

collisions has resulted from the investigations in either of these instances. Could the waves from the radar instruments have been the real cause? Perhaps Sidney A. Schneider has the answer.

As a young teenager, Sidney A. Schneider of Skokie, Illinois, became interested in hypnotism when he observed his older brother, a university student, successfully place his first subject under hypnosis. Sidney became an expert hypnotist. During his business career he became a radio operator and an engineer in electronics.

In the Second World War, Sidney Schneider was a vital part of the system known as 'I. F. F.'—Information, Friend or Foe. His job was to see to it that every ship leaving our country was equipped with radar. He noticed that radar operators sometimes went into a trance. They weren't aware that they had been in a trance when they came out of it.

Because of his knowledge of hypnosis and electronics, Schneider concluded that the fixed attention of the naval employees took place when the waves from the radar machine were synchronized with the brain waves of the operator. On this theory he changed the waves on the radar instrument and eliminated the recurrence of the trances.

Sidney Schneider told us that he converted his conclusions regarding the principle that placed the seamen operating radar in a trance into the Brain Wave Synchronizer, a machine which he invented after the war.

BRAIN WAVE SYNCHRONIZER

What is the Brain Wave Synchronizer?

It is an electronic instrument designed to induce various levels of hypnosis by subliminal and photic (light) stimulation of the brain waves. The instrument can be used alone or combined with a tape recording of the therapist's verbal suggestions. No physical connections or attachments are placed on the patient. Results are obtained at any distance in which the light in the machine is visible. The apparatus induces light to deep hypnotic levels in over 90 per cent of the subjects in an average time of three minutes.

In an experiment with the Brain Wave Synchronizer, none of the persons involved was informed about the machine or what it could do. Neither were they told that they were subjects of an experiment. Yet 30 per cent of them were hypnotized to various degrees, ranging from light to deep states.

'Why and how does the Brain Wave Synchronizer work?' we asked.

'It is like a television transmitter,' Schneider said. 'The human brain produces pulses (waves) of electricity in several frequency ranges. This knowledge has been applied in the field of medicine since 1929 and the invention of the electroencephalograph commonly known as the EEG machine, an apparatus for recording brain waves.

'My machine operates much like a television system,' Schneider continued. 'The reason the picture on your receiving set does not drift up or down is that the pulses generated within the set synchronize with corresponding pulses generated by the transmitting television station. The receiver is forced to operate at a rate controlled by the transmitter and the picture must obey.

'Like the transmitter of a television station, the Brain Wave Synchronizer also produces synchronizing pulses. And through photic stimulation, the waves sent from the synchronizer cause the frequency of the brain waves also to lock in step. At this point hypnosis can be achieved.

'Just compare your brain to a receiving set, and the Brain

Wave Synchronizer to a television transmitter.'

And you will see as you continue to read that in addition to comparing your brain to a receiving set, you can compare it to a television transmitter also.

A little knowledge becomes a dangerous thing. We have just explored some of the unseen forces from known physical causes. Now let's proceed further into the realm of the unknown: the thrilling field of psychic phenomena, such as:

1. ESP (extrasensory perception): awareness of or response to an external event or influence not apprehended by sensory means. Here are included:
   (a) Telepathy: thought transference
   (b) Clairvoyance: the power of discerning objects not present to the senses
   (c) Precognition: seeing into the future
   (d) Postcognition: seeing into the past
2. Psychokinesis: the effect of the mind on an object.

Now let's be realistic and keep our feet firmly on the ground. Let's explore the unknown with common sense! You'll be in danger unless you use good logic and avoid the gathering of cobwebs in your thinking. Facts should be your stepping-stones over the river of doubt. Therefore, let an experienced guide direct you along safe paths. And we will introduce you to such a guide. But before we do, let's talk about the past.

Thomas J. Hudson's famous book, *The Law of Psychic Phenomena*, when published in 1893, became a best seller. (The book is published today in paperback by Kessinger Publishing, White-fish, Montana.) It contained many thrilling stories of reported psychic experiences. The imaginations of tens of thousands of people who read this book were stimulated. Some were ready. Some were not.

From then on public interest in psychic phenomena made rapid progress. But many persons, not properly prepared, injured themselves by becoming crackpots. This was due to the awesomeness and magnetic interest a little knowledge of psychic powers generated within them. There is a noticeable tendency of some persons who are not properly educated and mature in their thinking and not very well adjusted emotionally to become fascinated with this intriguing study. It is easy to understand why so many religious leaders, scientists and persons responsible for the welfare of the people found the study of psychic phenomena an anathema:

1. Imaginations ran rampant and threatened the sanity of the people.
2. Fact and fiction seemed to be indistinguishable.
3. Hypnotism by amateurs and vaudeville entertainers, as well as the trickery and frauds practiced by fakirs, mediums and charlatans abused the minds of the public.
4. Basic religious principles were twisted in a direction that led to evil.

Anything associated with psychic phenomena became repellent. It was taboo.

In spite of the dangers, taboos and social or professional ostracism, there were courageous, honourable men with good common sense who had the courage to explore for the truth.

But it remained for the long, courageous fight of Dr Joseph Banks Rhine, formerly of Duke University, inspired and assisted by his wife Dr Louisa E. Rhine, to clothe the study of psychic phenomena with respectability. This is due to the impeccable character of Dr Rhine and to his 30 years of controlled laboratory experiments based on mathematical laws. His task was a difficult one because spontaneous psychic phenomena are not apt to occur in a laboratory. Such phenomena occur when least expected, most often when a person is under the greatest emotional strain, or possessed of an intensified obsessional desire—often simultaneously with the death of a loved one.

Westinghouse invests in ESP communication. It is apparent that any writer on the subject of psychic phenomena today endeavours to have the protection of a part of the cloak of Dr Rhine's respectability by referring to Dr Rhine and Duke University to make his own theories digestible. We are no exception. We urgently suggest that if you are interested further, you read *The Reach of the Mind* and the other books of which Dr Rhine is the author or co-author. Our recommendation: let Dr Joseph Banks Rhine be your guide.

And how successful has Dr Rhine's work been in breaking down the resistance to investigation and belief in these strange mindpowers? A fair test, it would seem to us, lies in the fact that hard-headed businessmen are convinced and are making experiments of their own. In an interview, Dr Peter A. Castruccio, Director of the Westinghouse Astronautics Institute, confirmed that Westinghouse scientists are engaged in research to find a means of using telepathy and clairvoyance for long distance communication. Dr Castruccio too had many lengthy visits with Dr Rhine before a decision was reached to engage in this great experiment.

And will the search for ways and means to harness telepathy and clairvoyance and make them commercially feasible be successful? Let us answer this as follows: Not too long ago, people were scoffing at ideas that were unbelievable to them then but are taken for granted today: (a) matter being turned into energy and energy into matter; (b) the breaking of the atom; (c) man-made satellites; (d) jet power; or (e) everyday necessities like television, for example.

And what about the electronic computer that was designed from the human computer: the human brain and the nervous system. Every one was conceived, believed and achieved by men with PMA! Machines that operate with the speed of light—186,300 miles per second! Machines that can calculate 40,000 arithmetical operations per second and detect and correct their own errors! Machines that became a reality because man built into them electrical circuits which in many respects function like the known electrical activity of the nervous system of your own physical body. Our answer: what the mind of man can conceive and believe, the mind of man can achieve with PMA!

But no machine or man-made invention is as marvellous as the wonderful human computer you own: your brain and your nervous system, with their power of electrical activity.

Man is more than a body with a brain.

You are a mind with a body—a mind, possessing, and also affected by, powers known and unknown! A mind composed of two parts: the conscious and the subconscious.

Here we have stressed most the concept of the subconscious mind—its powers and the forces known and unknown that affect it. But what about the conscious mind? That is equally important.

Now, if your reaction to what you have read has not given you an insight on how you can turn the right knob or push the right button to get what you want from the machine you own, dare to explore the powers of your mind.

POINTS TO REMEMBER

1. Exploring the powers of your mind can bring you long lasting happiness and wealth.
2. It is most important that you read aloud the statement of your desire.
3. The potent effect of unseen forces.

3

A DEFINITE CHIEF AIM

Singleness of purpose is essential for success, no matter what may be one's idea of the definition of success. Yet singleness of purpose is a quality which may, and generally does, call for thought on many allied subjects.

A well organized, alert and energetic mind is produced by various and sundry stimuli, all of which are plainly described in these lessons.

It should be remembered, however, that the mind requires, for its development, a variety of exercise, just as the physical body, to be properly developed, calls for many forms of systematic exercise.

Horses are trained to certain gaits by trainers who hurdle-jump them over handicaps which cause them to develop the desired steps, through habit and repetition. The human mind must be trained in a similar manner, by a variety of thought-inspiring stimuli.

You will observe, before you have gone very far into this philosophy, that the reading of these lessons will super induce a flow of thoughts covering a wide range of subjects. For this reason, the student should read the course with a notebook and pencil at hand, and follow the practice of recording these thoughts or 'ideas' as they come into the mind.

By following this suggestion the student will have a collection of ideas, by the time the course has been read two or three times, sufficient to transform his or her entire life-plan.

By following this practice, it will be noticed, very soon, that the mind has become like a magnet in that it will attract useful ideas right out of the 'thin air', to use the words of a noted scientist who has experimented with this principle for a great number of years.

You will do yourself a great injustice if you undertake this course with even a remote feeling that you do not stand in need of more knowledge than you now possess. In truth, no man knows enough about any worthwhile subject to entitle him to feel that he has the last word on that subject.

In the long, hard task of trying to wipe out some of my own ignorance and make way for some of the useful truths of life, I have often seen, in my imagination, the Great Marker who stands at the gateway entrance of life and writes 'Poor Fool' on the brow of those who believe they are wise, and 'Poor Sinner' on the brow of those who believe they are saints.

Which, translated into workaday language, means that none of us know very much, and by the very nature of our being can never know as much as we need to know in order to live sanely and enjoy life while we live.

Humility is a forerunner of success!

Until we become humble in our own hearts we are not apt to profit greatly by the experiences and thoughts of others.

Sounds like a preachment on morality? Well, what if it does?

Even 'preachments', as dry and lacking in interest as they generally are, may be beneficial if they serve to reflect the shadow of our real selves so we may get an approximate idea of our smallness and superficiality.

Success in life is largely predicated upon our knowing men!

The best place to study the man-animal is in your own mind, by taking as accurate an inventory as possible of YOURSELF. When you know yourself thoroughly (if you ever do) you will also know much about others.

To know others, not as they seem to be, but as they really are, study them through:

1. The posture of the body and the way they walk.
2. The tone of the voice, its quality, pitch, volume.
3. The eyes, whether shifty or direct.
4. The use of words, their trend, nature and quality.

This philosophy is intended to enable those who master it to 'sell' their way through life successfully, with the minimum amount of resistance and friction. Such a course, therefore, must help the student organize and make use of much truth which is overlooked by the majority of people who go through life as mediocres.

Not all people are so constituted that they wish to know the truth about all matters vitally affecting life. One of the great surprises the author of this course has met with, in connection with his research activities, is that so few people are willing to hear the truth when it shows up their own weaknesses.

We prefer illusions to realities!

New truths, if accepted at all, are taken with the proverbial grain of salt. Some of us demand more than a mere pinch of salt; we demand enough to pickle new ideas so they become useless.

For these reasons the Introductory Lesson of this course, and this lesson as well, cover subjects intended to pave the way for new ideas so those ideas will not be too severe a shock to the mind of the student.

RISKS ASSOCIATED WITH NEW IDEAS

The thought the author wishes to 'get across' has been quite plainly stated by the editor of the American Magazine, in an editorial which appeared in a recent issue, in the following words,

'On a recent rainy night, Carl Lomen, the reindeer king of Alaska, told me a true story. It has stuck in my crop ever since. And now I am going to pass it along.

"'A certain Greenland Eskimo" said Lomen, "was taken on one of the American North Polar expeditions a number of years ago. Later, as a reward for faithful service, he was brought to New York City for a short visit. At all the miracles of sight and sound he was filled with a most amazed wonder. When he returned to his native village he told stories of buildings that rose into the very face of the sky; of street cars, which he described as houses that moved along the trail, with people living in them as they moved; of mammoth bridges, artificial lights, and all the other dazzling concomitants of the metropolis.

"'His people looked at him coldly and walked away. And forthwith throughout the whole village he was dubbed "Sagdluk", meaning "the Liar," and this name he carried in shame to his grave. Long before his death his original name was entirely forgotten.

"'When Knud Rasmussen made his trip from Greenland to Alaska he was accompanied by a Greenland Eskimo named Mitek (Eider Duck). Mitek visited Copenhagen and New York, where he saw many things for the first time and was greatly impressed. Later, upon his return to Greenland, he recalled the tragedy of Sagdluk, and decided that it would not be wise to tell the truth. Instead, he would narrate stories that his people could grasp, and thus save his reputation.

"'So he told them how he and Doctor Rasmussen maintained a kayak on the banks of a great river, the Hudson, and how, each morning, they paddled out for their hunting. Ducks, geese and seals were to be had a-plenty, and they enjoyed the visit immensely.

"'Mitek, in the eyes of his countrymen, is a very honest man. His neighbours treat him with rare respect."

'The road of the truth-teller has always been rocky. Socrates sipping the hemlock, Christ crucified, Stephen stoned, Bruno burned at the stake, Galileo terrified into retraction of his starry truths—forever could one follow that bloody trail through the pages of history.

"Something in human nature makes us resent the impact of new ideas."

We hate to be disturbed in the beliefs and prejudices that have been handed down with the family furniture. At maturity too many of us go into hibernation, and live off the fat of ancient fetishes. If a new idea invades our den, we rise up snarling from our winter sleep.

The Eskimos, at least, had some excuse. They were unable to visualize the startling pictures drawn by Sagdluk. Their simple lives had been too long circumscribed by the brooding arctic night.

But there is no adequate reason why the average man should ever close his mind to fresh 'slants' on life. He does, just the same. Nothing is more tragic—or more common—than mental inertia. For every ten men who are physically lazy there are ten thousand with stagnant minds. And stagnant minds are the breeding places of fear.

An old farmer up in Vermont always used to wind up his prayers with this plea, 'Oh, God, give me an open mind!' If more people followed his example they might escape being hamstrung by prejudices. And what a pleasant place to live in the world would be.

◆

Every person should make it his business to gather new ideas from sources other than the environment in which he daily lives and works.

The mind becomes withered, stagnant, narrow and closed unless it searches for new ideas. The farmer should come to the city quite often, and walk among the strange faces and the tall buildings. He will go back to his farm, his mind refreshed, with more courage and greater enthusiasm.

The city man should take a trip to the country every so often and freshen his mind with sights new and different from those associated with his daily labours.

Everyone needs a change of mental environment at regular periods, the same as a change and variety of food are essential. The mind becomes more alert, more elastic and more ready to work with speed and accuracy after it has been bathed in new ideas, outside of one's own field of daily labour.

As a student of this course, you will temporarily lay aside the set of ideas with which you perform your daily labours, and enter a field of entirely new (and in some instances, heretofore unheard-of) ideas.

Splendid! You will come out, at the other end of this course, with a new stock of ideas which will make you more efficient, more enthusiastic and more courageous, no matter in what sort of work you may be engaged.

Do not be afraid of new ideas! They may mean to you the difference between success and failure.

> **POINTS TO REMEMBER**
>
> 1. Singleness of purpose is essential for success.
> 2. Exercise your mind just as you do for your physical body.
> 3. Until we become humble in our own hearts we are not apt to profit greatly.

4

CONCENTRATION

This lesson occupies a keystone position in this course, for the reason that the psychological law upon which it is based is of vital importance to every other lesson of the course.

Let us define the word *concentration*, as it is here used, as follows: *concentration is the act of focussing the mind upon a given desire until ways and means for its realisation have been worked out and successfully put into operation.* Two important laws enter into the act of concentrating the mind on a given desire. One is the law of autosuggestion and the other is the law of habit. The former having been fully described in a previous lesson of this course, we will now briefly describe the law of habit.

Habit grows out of environment—out of doing the same thing in the same way over and over again—out of repetition—out of thinking the same thoughts over and over—and, when once formed, it resembles a cement block that has hardened in the mould—in that it is hard to break.

Habit is the basis of all memory training, a fact which you may easily demonstrate in remembering the name of a person whom you have just met, by repeating that name over and over until you have fixed it permanently and plainly in your mind. 'The force of education is so great that we may mould the minds and manners of the young into whatever shape we please and give the impressions of such habits as shall ever afterwards remain.'—Atterbury.

Except on rare occasions when the mind rises above environment, the human mind draws the material out of which thought is created, from the surrounding environment, and habit crystallizes this thought into a permanent fixture and stores it away in the subconscious mind where it becomes a vital part of our personality which silently influences our actions, forms our prejudices and our biases and controls our opinions. A great philosopher had in mind the power of habit when he said, 'We first endure, then pity and finally embrace,' in speaking of the manner in which honest men come to indulge in crime.

Habit may be likened to the grooves on a phonograph record, while the mind may be likened to the needle point that fits into that groove. When any habit has been well formed (by repetition of thought or action) the mind attaches itself to and follows that habit as closely as the phonograph needle follows the groove in the wax record, no matter what may be the nature of that habit.

We begin to see, therefore, the importance of selecting our environment with the greatest of care, because environment is the mental feeding ground out of which the food that goes into our minds is extracted.

Environment very largely supplies the food and materials out of which we create thought, and habit crystallizes these into permanency. You of course understand that 'environment' is the sum total of sources through which you are influenced by and through the aid of the five senses of seeing, hearing, smelling, tasting and feeling.

'Habit is force which is generally recognized by the average thinking person, but which is commonly viewed in its adverse aspect to the exclusion of its favourable phase. It has been well said that all men are "the creatures of habit", and that "habit is a cable; we weave a thread of it each day and it becomes so strong that we cannot break it."

'If it be true that habit becomes a cruel tyrant, ruling and compelling men against their will, desire and inclination—and this is true in many cases—the question naturally arises in the thinking mind whether this mighty force cannot be harnessed and controlled in the service of men, just as have other forces of Nature. If this result can be accomplished, then man may master habit and set it to work, instead of being a slave to it and serving it faithfully though complaining. And the modern psychologists tell us in no uncertain tones that habit may certainly be thus mastered, harnessed and set to work, instead of being allowed to dominate one's actions and character. And thousands of people have applied this new knowledge and have turned the force of habit into new channels, and have compelled it to work their machinery of action, instead of being allowed to run to waste, or else permitted to sweep away the structures that men have erected with care and expense, or to destroy fertile mental fields.

'A habit is a "mental path" over which our actions have travelled for some time, each passing making the path a little deeper and a little wider. If you have to walk over a field or through a forest, you know how natural it is for you to choose the clearest path in preference to the less worn ones, and greatly in preference to stepping out across the field or through the woods and making a new path. And the line of mental action is precisely the same. It is movement along the lines of least resistance—passage over the well-worn path. Habits are created by repetition and are formed in accordance to a natural law, observable in all animate things and some would say in inanimate things as well. As an instance of the latter, it is pointed out that a piece of paper once folded in a certain way will fold along the same lines the next time. And all users of sewing machines, or other delicate pieces of machinery, know that as a machine or instrument is once "broken in" so will it tend to run thereafter. The same law is also observable in the case of musical instruments. Clothing or gloves form into creases according to the person using them, and these creases once formed will always be in effect, notwithstanding repeated pressings. Rivers and streams of water cut their courses through the land, and thereafter flow along the habit-course. The law is in operation everywhere.

'These illustrations will help you to form the idea of the nature of habit, and will aid you in forming new mental paths— new mental creases. And—remember this always—the best (and one might say the only) way in which old habits may be removed is to form new habits to counteract and replace the undesirable ones. Form new mental paths over which to travel, and the old ones will soon become less distinct and in time will practically fill up from disuse. Every time you travel over the path of the desirable mental habit, you make the path deeper and wider, and make it so much easier to travel it thereafter. This mental path-making is a very important thing, and I cannot urge upon you too strongly the injunction to start to work making the desirable mental paths over which you wish to travel. Practice, practice, practice—be a good path-maker.'

The following are the rules of procedure through which you may form the habits you desire:

First: at the beginning of the formation of a new habit put force and enthusiasm into your expression. Feel what you think.

Remember that you are taking the first steps toward making the new mental path; that it is much harder at first than it will be afterwards. Make the path as clear and as deep as you can, at the beginning, so that you can readily see it the next time you wish to follow it.

Second: keep your attention firmly concentrated on the new path-building, and keep your mind away from the old paths, lest you incline toward them. Forget all about the old paths, and concern yourself only with the new ones that you are building to order.

Third: travel over your newly made paths as often as possible. Make opportunities for doing so, without waiting for them to arise through luck or chance. The oftener you go over the new paths the sooner will they become well-worn and easily travelled. Create plans for passing over these new habit-paths, at the very start.

Fourth: resist the temptation to travel over the older, easier paths that you have been using in the past. Every time you resist a temptation, the stronger do you become, and the easier will it be for you to do so the next time. But every time you yield to the temptation, the easier does it become to yield again, and the more difficult it becomes to resist the next time. You will have a fight on at the start, and this is the critical time. Prove your determination, persistency and willpower now, at the very beginning.

Fifth: be sure that you have mapped out the right path, as your definite chief aim, and then go ahead without fear and without allowing yourself to doubt. 'Place your hand upon the plough, and look not backward.' Select your goal, then make good, deep, wide mental paths leading straight to it.

As you have already observed, there is a close relationship between habit and autosuggestion (self-suggestion). Through habit, an act repeatedly performed in the same manner has a tendency to become permanent, and eventually we come to perform the act automatically or unconsciously. In playing a piano, for example, the artist can play a familiar piece while his or her conscious mind is on some other subject.

Autosuggestion is the tool with which we dig a mental path; Concentration is the hand that holds that tool; and Habit is the map or blueprint which the mental path follows. An idea or desire, to be transformed into terms of action or physical reality, must be held in the conscious mind faithfully and persistently until habit begins to give it permanent form.

Let us turn our attention, now, to environment.

As we have already seen, we absorb the material for thought from our surrounding environment. The term 'environment' covers a very broad field. It consists of the books we read, the people with whom we associate, the community in which we live, the nature of the work in which we are engaged, the country or nation in which we reside, the clothes we wear, the songs we sing and, most important of all, the religious and intellectual training we receive prior to the age of fourteen years.

The purpose of analysing the subject of environment is to show its direct relationship to the personality we are developing, and the importance of so guarding it that its influence will give us the materials out of which we may attain our definite chief aim in life.

The mind feeds upon that which we supply it, or that which is forced upon it, through our *environment;* therefore, let us select our environment, as far as possible, with the object of supplying the mind with suitable material out of which to carry on its work of attaining our *definite chief aim.*

If *your* environment is not to your liking, change it!

The first step is to create in your own mind an exact, clear and well rounded out picture of the environment in which you believe you could best attain your *definite chief aim,* and then *concentrate* your mind upon this picture until you transform it into reality.

The first step you must take, in the accomplishment of any *desire,* is to create in your mind a clear, well defined picture of that which you intend to accomplish. This is the first principle to be observed in your plans for the achievement of *success,* and if you fail or neglect to observe it, you cannot succeed, except by chance.

Your daily associates constitute one of the most important and influential parts of your environment, and may work for your progress or your retrogression, according to the nature of those associates. As far as possible, you should select as your most *intimate* daily associates those who are in sympathy with your aims and ideals—especially those represented by your *definite chief aim*—and whose mental attitude inspires you with enthusiasm, self-confidence, determination and ambition.

Remember that every word spoken within your hearing, every sight that reaches your eyes and every sense impression that you receive through any of the five senses, influences your thought as surely as the sun rises in the east and sets in the west. This being true, can you not see the importance of controlling, as far as possible, the environment in which you live and work? Can you not see the importance of reading books that deal with subjects which are directly related to your *definite chief aim?* Can you not see the importance of talking with people who are in sympathy with your aims, and, who will encourage you and spur you on toward their attainment? We are living in what we call a 'twentieth century civilization'. The leading scientists of the world are agreed that Nature has been millions of years in creating, through the process of evolution, our present civilized environment.

How many hundreds of centuries the so-called Indians had lived upon the North American continent, without any appreciable advance toward modem civilization, as we understand it, we have no way of ascertaining. Their environment was the wilderness, and they made no attempt whatsoever to change or improve that environment; the change took place only after new races from afar came over and *forced upon them the environment of progressive civilisation in, which we are living today.*

DIRECTLY PROPORTIONAL RELATION OF THE MIND WITH ONE'S SURROUNDINGS

Observe what has happened within the short period of three centuries. Hunting grounds have been transformed into great cities, and the Indian has taken on education and culture, in many instances, that equal the accomplishment of his white brothers.

The clothes you wear influence you; therefore, they constitute a part of your environment. Soiled or shabby clothes depress you and lower your self-confidence, while clean clothes, of an appropriate style, have just the opposite effect.

It is a well-known fact that an observant person can accurately analyse a man by seeing his workbench, desk or other place of employment. A well-organized desk indicates a well-organized brain. Show me the merchant's stock of goods and I will tell you whether he has an organized or disorganized brain, as there is a close relationship between one's mental attitude and one's physical environment.

The effects of environment so vitally influence those who work in factories, stores and offices, that employers are gradually realizing the importance of creating an environment that inspires and encourages the workers.

One unusually progressive laundryman, in the city of Chicago, has plainly outdone his competitors, by installing in his workroom a player-piano, in charge of a neatly dressed young woman who keeps it going during the working hours. His laundrywomen are dressed in white uniforms, and there is no evidence about the place that work is drudgery. Through the aid of this pleasant environment, this laundryman turns out more work, earns more profits and pays better wages than his competitors can pay.

This brings us to an appropriate place at which to describe the method through which you may apply the principles directly and indirectly related to the subject of concentration.

This key that is used, in one form or another, by the followers of New Thought and all other sects which are founded upon the positive philosophy of optimism.

This Magic Key constitutes an irresistible power which all who will may use.

It will unlock the door to riches! It will unlock the door to fame!

And, in many instances, it will unlock the door to physical health.

It will unlock the door to education and let you into the storehouse of all your latent ability. It will act as a pass-key to any position in life for which you are fitted.

Through the aid of this Magic Key we have unlocked the secret doors to all of the world's great inventions.

Through its magic powers all of our great geniuses of the past have been developed.

Suppose you are a labourer, in a menial position, and desire a better place in life. The Magic Key will help you attain it! Through its use Carnegie, Rockefeller, Hill, Harriman, Morgan and scores of others of their type have accumulated vast fortunes of material wealth.

It will unlock prison doors and turn human derelicts into useful, trustworthy human beings. It will turn failure into success and misery into happiness. You ask, 'What is this Magic Key?'

And I answer with one word, 'concentration!' Now let me define concentration in the sense that it is here used. First, I wish it to be clearly understood that I have no reference to occultism, although I will admit that all the scientists of the world have failed to explain the strange phenomena produced through the aid of concentration.

Concentration, in the sense in which it is here used, means the ability, through fixed habit and practice, to keep your mind on one subject until you have thoroughly familiarized yourself with that subject and mastered it. It means the ability to control your attention and focus it on a given problem until you have solved it.

It means the ability to throw off the effects of habits which you wish to discard, and the power to build new habits that are more to your liking. It means complete self-mastery.

Stating it in another way, concentration is the ability to think as you wish to think; the ability to control your thoughts and direct them to a definite end; and the ability to organize your knowledge into a plan of action that is sound and workable.

You can readily see that in concentrating your mind upon your definite chief aim in life, you must cover many closely related subjects which blend into each other and complete the main subject upon which you are concentrating.

Ambition and desire are the chief factors which enter into the act of successful concentration. Without these factors the Magic Key is useless, and the main reason why so few people make use of this key is that most people lack ambition, and desire nothing in particular.

Desire whatever you may, and if your desire is within reason and if it is strong enough the Magic Key of concentration will help you attain it. There are learned men of science who would have us believe that the wonderful power of prayer operates through the principle of concentration on the attainment of a deeply seated desire.

Nothing was ever created by a human being which was not first created in the imagination, through desire, and then transformed into reality through concentration.

Now, let us put the Magic Key to a test, through the aid of a definite formula.

First, you must put your foot on the neck of scepticism and doubt! No unbeliever ever enjoyed the benefits of this Magic Key. You must believe in the test that you are about to make.

We will assume that you have thought something about becoming a successful writer or a powerful public speaker or a successful business executive or an able financier. We will take public speaking as the subject of this test, but remember that you must follow instructions to the letter.

Take a plain sheet of paper, ordinary letter size and write on it the following:

> I am going to become a powerful public speaker because this will enable me to render the world useful service that is needed—and because it will yield me a financial return that will provide me with the necessary material things of life.

I will concentrate my mind upon this desire for ten minutes daily, just before retiring at night and just after arising in the morning, for the purpose of determining just how I shall proceed to transform it into reality.

I know that I can become a powerful and magnetic speaker, therefore I will permit nothing to interfere with my doing so.

Signed ....

Sign this pledge, then proceed to do as you have pledged your word that you would do. Keep it up until the desired results have been realized.

Now, when you come to do your concentrating, this is the way to go about it: look ahead one, three, five or even ten years, and see yourself as the most powerful speaker of your time. See, in your imagination, an appropriate income. See yourself in your own home that you have purchased with the proceeds from your efforts as a speaker or lecturer. See yourself in possession of a nice bank account as a reserve for old age. See yourself as a person of influence, due to your great ability as a public speaker. See yourself engaged in a life-calling in which you will not fear the loss of your position.

Paint this picture clearly, through the powers of your imagination, and lo! it will soon become transformed into a beautiful picture of deeply seated desire. Use this desire as the chief object of your concentration and observe what happens.

You now have the secret of the Magic Key!

Do not underestimate the power of the Magic Key because it did not come to you clothed in mysticism, or because it is described in language which all who will may understand. All great truths are simple in final analysis, and easily understood;

if they are not they are not great truths.

Use this Magic Key with intelligence, and only for the attainment of worthy ends, and it will bring you enduring happiness and success. Forget the mistakes you have made and the failures you have experienced. Quit living in the past, for do you not know that your yesterdays never return? Start all over again, if your previous efforts have not turned out well, and make the next five or ten years tell a story of success that will satisfy your most lofty ambitions.

Make a name for yourself and render the world a great service, through ambition, desire and concentrated effort!

You can do it if you BELIEVE you can!

Thus endeth the Magic Key.

The presence of any idea or thought in your consciousness tends to produce an 'associated' feeling and to urge you to appropriate or corresponding action. Hold a deeply seated desire in your consciousness, through the principle of concentration, and if you do it with full faith in its realization your act attracts to your aid powers which the entire scientific world has failed to understand or explain with a reasonable hypothesis.

When you become familiar with the powers of concentration you will then understand the reason for choosing a definite chief aim as the first step in the attainment of enduring success.

Concentrate your mind upon the attainment of the object of a deeply seated desire and very soon you will become a lodestone that attracts, through the aid of forces which no man can explain, the necessary material counterparts of that desire, a statement of fact which paves the way for the description of a principle which constitutes the most important part of this lesson, if not, in fact, the most important part of the entire course, viz.:

When two or more people ally themselves, in a spirit of perfect harmony, for the purpose of attaining a definite end, if that alliance is faithfully observed by all of whom it is composed, the alliance brings, to each of those of whom it is composed, power that is superhuman and seemingly irresistible in nature.

ATTAINMENT OF YOUR ZENITH

In chemistry we learn that two or more elements may be so compounded that the result is something entirely different in nature, from any of the individual elements. For example, ordinary water, known in chemistry under the formula of H_2O, is a compound consisting of two atoms of hydrogen and one atom of oxygen, but water is neither hydrogen nor oxygen. This 'marrying' of elements creates an entirely different substance from that of either of its component parts.

The same law through which this transformation of physical elements takes place may be responsible for the seemingly superhuman powers resulting from the alliance of two or more people, in a perfect state of harmony and understanding, for the attainment of a given end.

This world, and all matter of which the other planets consist, is made up of electrons (an electron being the smallest known analysable unit of matter, and resembling, in nature, what we call electricity, or a form of energy). On the other hand, thought, and that which we call the 'mind', is also a form of energy; in fact it is the highest form of energy known.

Thought, in other words, is organised energy, and it is not improbable that thought is exactly the same sort of energy as that which we generate with an electric dynamo, although of a much more highly organised form.

Now, if all matter, in final analysis, consists of groups of electrons, which are nothing more than a form of energy which we call electricity, and if the mind is nothing but a form of highly organized electricity, do you not see how it is possible that the laws which affect matter may also govern the mind?

And if combining two or more elements of matter, in the proper proportion and under the right conditions, will produce something entirely different from those original elements (as in the case of H_2O), do you not see how it is possible so to combine the energy of two or more minds that the result will be a sort of composite mind that is totally different from the individual minds of which it consists?

You have undoubtedly noticed the manner in which; you are influenced while in the presence of other people. Some people inspire you with optimism and enthusiasm. Their very presence seems to stimulate your own mind to greater action, and, this not only 'seems' to be true, but it is true. You have noticed that the presence of others had a tendency to lower your vitality and depress you; a tendency which I can assure you was very real!

What, do you imagine, could be the cause of these changes that come over us when we come within a certain range of other people, unless it is the change resulting from the blending or combining of their minds with our own, through the operation of a law that is not very well understood, but resembles (if, in fact, it is not the same law) the law through which the combining of two atoms of hydrogen and one atom of oxygen produces water.

I have no scientific basis for this hypothesis, but I have given it many years of serious thought and always I come to the conclusion that it is at least a sound hypothesis, although I have no possible way, as yet, of reducing it to a provable hypothesis.

You need no proof, however, that the presence of some people inspires you, while the presence of others depresses you, as you know this to be a fact. Now it stands to reason that the person who inspires you and arouses your mind to a state of greater activity gives you more power to achieve, while the person whose presence depresses you and lowers your vitality, or causes you to dissipate it in useless, disorganized thought, has just the opposite effect on you. You can understand this much without the aid of a hypothesis and without further proof than that which you have experienced time after time. Come back, now, to the original statement that,

'When two or more people ally themselves, *in a spirit of perfect harmony,* for the purpose of attaining a definite end, if that alliance is *faithfully observed by all of whom it is composed,* the alliance brings, to each of those of whom it is composed, power that is superhuman and seemingly irresistible in nature.'

Study, closely, the emphasized part of the foregoing statement, for there you will find the 'mental formula' which, if not faithfully observed, destroys the effect of the whole.

One atom of hydrogen combined with one atom of oxygen will not produce water, nor will an alliance in name only, that is not accompanied by 'a spirit of perfect harmony' (between those forming the alliance), produce 'power that is superhuman and seemingly irresistible in nature.'

I have in mind a family of mountain-folk who, for more than six generations, have lived in the mountainous section of Kentucky. Generation after generation of this family came and went without any noticeable improvement of a mental nature, each generation following in the footsteps of its ancestors. They made their living from the soil, and as far as they knew, or cared, the universe consisted of a little spot of territory known as Letcher County. They married strictly in their own 'set', and in their own community.

Finally, one of the members of this family strayed away from the flock, so to speak, and married a well-educated and highly cultured woman from the neighbour-state of Virginia. This woman was one of those types of ambitious people who had learned that the universe extended beyond the border line of Letcher County, and covered, at least, the whole of the southern states. She had heard of chemistry, and of botany, and of biology, and of pathology, and of psychology and of many other subjects that were of importance in the field of education. When her children began to come along to the age of understanding, she talked to them of these subjects; and they, in turn, began to show a keen interest in them.

One of her children is now the president of a great educational institution, where most of these subjects, and many others of equal importance, are taught. Another one of them is a prominent lawyer, while still another is a successful physician.

Her husband (thanks to the influence of her mind) is a well-known dental surgeon, and the first of his family, for six generations, to break away from the traditions by which the family had been bound.

The blending of her mind with his gave him the needed stimulus to spur him on and inspired him with ambition such as he would never have known without her influence.

For many years I have been studying the biographies of those whom the world calls great, and it seems to me more than a mere coincidence that in every instance where the facts were available the person who was really responsible for the *greatness* was in the background, behind the scenes, and seldom heard of by the hero-worshiping public. Not infrequently is this 'hidden power' a patient little wife who has inspired her husband and urged him on to great achievement, as was true in the case I have just described.

Henry Ford is one of the modem miracles of this age, and I doubt that this country, or any other, ever produced an industrial genius of his equal. If the facts were known (and perhaps they are known) they might trace the cause of Mr Ford's phenomenal achievements to a woman of whom the public hears but little—his wife!

We read of Ford's achievements and of his enormous income and imagine him to be blessed with matchless ability; and he is— ability of which the world would never have heard had it not been for the modifying influence of his wife, who has cooperated with him, during all the years of his struggle, 'in a spirit of perfect harmony, for the purpose of attaining a definite end.'

When two or more people ally themselves, 'in a spirit of perfect harmony, for the purpose of attaining a definite end,' the *end*, itself, or the *desire* back of that end, may be likened to the apple seed, and the blending of the forces of energy of the two or more minds may be likened to the air and the soil out of which come the elements that form the material objects of that *desire*.

The power back of the attraction and combination of these forces of the mind can no more be explained than can the power back of the combination of elements out of which an apple tree 'grows'.

But the all-important thing is that an apple tree will 'grow' from a seed thus properly planted, a great *achievement* will follow the systematic blending of two or more minds with a definite object in view.

POINTS TO REMEMBER

1. The law of autosuggestion and the law of habit are necessary in order to learn how to concentrate well.
2. Habit is the basis of cultivating a good memory.
3. Setting up a definite chief aim is the most important step towards attaining success.

5

IMAGINATION

The Imagination is literally the workshop wherein are fashioned all plans created by humankind. The impulse, the DESIRE, is given shape, form, and ACTION through the aid of the imaginative faculty of the mind.

It has been said that anything can be created which a human being can imagine.

Of all the ages of civilization, the one in which we live is the most favourable for the development of the imagination because it is an age of rapid change. On every hand we may contact stimuli which develop the imagination.

Through the aid of the imaginative faculty, we have discovered, and harnessed, more of Nature's forces during the past fifty years than during the entire history of the human race previous to that time. We have conquered the air so completely that the birds are a poor match for us in flying. We have harnessed the electromagnetic spectrum and made it serve as a means of instantaneous communication with any part of the world. We have analysed and weighed the sun at a distance of millions of miles and determined through the aid of IMAGINATION the elements of which it consists. We have discovered that our own brains are both a broadcasting and a receiving station for the 'vibration of thought', although we have only barely begun to understand this phenomenon with the aim of making practical use of this discovery. We have increased the speed of travel until we may now breakfast in New York and lunch in San Francisco.

OUR ONLY LIMITATION, within reason, LIES IN OUR DEVELOPMENT AND USE OF OUR IMAGINATION. We have not yet reached the apex of development in the use of the 'imaginative faculty'. We have merely discovered that we have an imagination, and have commenced to use it only in a very elementary way.

TWO FORMS OF IMAGINATION

The imaginative faculty functions in two forms. One is known as Synthetic Imagination and the other as Creative Imagination.

SYNTHETIC IMAGINATION—through this faculty, one can arrange old concepts, ideas or plans into new combinations. This faculty *creates* nothing. It merely works with the material of experience, education and observation with which it is fed. It is the faculty used most by the inventor —with the exception of the genius, who draws upon the Creative Imagination when unable to solve a problem through Synthetic Imagination.

CREATIVE IMAGINATION—through the faculty of Creative Imagination, the finite human mind has direct communication with Infinite Intelligence. It is the faculty through which 'hunches' and 'inspirations' are received. It is by this faculty that all basic or new ideas are handed over to us. It is through this faculty that 'thought vibrations' or 'influences' from the minds of others are received. It is through this faculty that one individual may 'tune in' or communicate with the subconscious minds of others.

The Creative Imagination works automatically in the manner

described in subsequent pages. This faculty functions ONLY when the conscious mind is functioning at an exceedingly high level of 'intensity' or 'energy', as for example, when the conscious mind is stimulated through the emotion of a *strong desire*.

The Creative Imagination becomes more alert, more receptive to influences from the sources mentioned, in proportion to its development through USE. This statement is significant! Ponder over it before passing on.

Keep in mind as you follow these principles that the entire story of how one may convert DESIRE into money cannot be told in one statement. The story will be complete only when one has MASTERED, ASSIMILATED and BEGUN TO MAKE USE of *all* the success principles that are explained, and tied together, in this book.

The great leaders of business, industry, finance and the great artists, musicians, poets and writers became great because they developed the faculty of Creative Imagination.

Both the synthetic and creative faculties of imagination become more alert with use, just as any muscle or organ of the body develops through use.

Desire is only a thought, an impulse. It is nebulous and ephemeral. It is abstract, and of no value, until it has been transformed into its physical counterpart. While the Synthetic Imagination is the one which will be used most frequently in the process of transforming the impulse of DESIRE into money, you must keep in mind the fact that you may face circumstances and situations which demand the use of the Creative Imagination as well.

Your imaginative faculty may have become weak through inaction. It can be revived and made alert through USE. This faculty does not die, though it may become dormant through lack of use.

Centre your attention, for the time being, on developing the Synthetic Imagination because this is the faculty which you will use more often in the process of converting desire into money.

Transforming the intangible impulse of DESIRE into the tangible reality of MONEY calls for the use of a plan or plans. These plans must be formed with the aid of the imagination, mainly Synthetic Imagination.

Read this entire book through, then come back to this chapter and begin at once to put your imagination to work on building a plan or plans to transform your DESIRE into money. Detailed instructions for building plans have been given in almost every chapter. Carry out the instructions best suited to your needs, and reduce your plan to writing if you have not already done so. The moment you complete this, you will have DEFINITELY given concrete form to the intangible DESIRE. Read the preceding sentence once more. Read it aloud, very slowly, and as you do so, remember that the moment you reduce the statement of your desire—and a plan for its realization—to writing, you have actually TAKEN THE FIRST of a series of steps which will enable you to convert the thought into its physical counterpart.

The earth on which you live, you yourself, and every other material thing are the result of evolutionary change—through which microscopic bits of matter have been organized and arranged in an orderly fashion.

Moreover—and this statement is of stupendous importance—this earth, every one of the billions of individual cells of your body, and every atom of matter began as an intangible form of energy.

DESIRE is thought impulse! Thought impulses are forms of

energy. When you begin with the thought impulse of DESIRE TO ACCUMULATE MONEY or any other object of desire, you are drafting into your service the same stuff that Nature used in creating this earth and every material form in the universe, including the body and brain in which the thought impulses function.

As far as science has been able to determine, the entire universe consists of but two elements—matter and energy.

Through the combination of energy and matter has been created everything which we can perceive, from the largest star which floats in the heavens down to and including ourselves.

You are now engaged in the task of trying to profit by Nature's method. You are (sincerely and earnestly, we hope) trying to adapt yourself to Nature's laws by endeavouring to convert DESIRE into its physical or monetary equivalent. YOU CAN DO IT! IT HAS BEEN DONE BEFORE!

You can build a fortune through the aid of laws which are immutable. But first you must become familiar with these laws and learn to USE them. Through repetition, and by approaching the description of these principles from every conceivable angle, I hope to reveal to you the secret through which every great fortune has been accumulated. Strange and paradoxical as it may seem, the secret is NOT A SECRET. Nature herself advertises it in the earth on which we live, the stars, the planets suspended within our view, in the elements above and around us, in every blade of grass, and in every form of life within our vision.

Nature advertises this secret in the terms of biology, in the conversion of a tiny cell, so small that it may be lost on the point of a pin, into the HUMAN BEING now reading this line. The conversion of desire into its physical equivalent is certainly no more miraculous!

Do not become discouraged if you do not fully comprehend all that has been stated. Unless you have long been a student of the mind, it is not to be expected that you will assimilate all that is in this chapter upon a first reading.

But you will, in time, make good progress.

The principles that follow will open the way for understanding of imagination. Assimilate that which you understand as you read this philosophy for the first time, then when you reread and study it, you will discover that something has happened to clarify it and give you a broader understanding of the whole. Above all, DO NOT STOP nor hesitate in your study of these principles until you have read the book at least THREE times —for then you will not want to stop.

HOW TO MAKE PRACTICAL USE OF IMAGINATION

Ideas are the beginning points of all fortunes. Ideas are products of the imagination. Let us examine a few well-known ideas which have yielded huge fortunes, with the hope that these illustrations will convey definite information concerning the method by which imagination may be used in accumulating riches.

The Enchanted Kettle

Fifty years ago, an old country doctor drove to town, hitched his horse, quietly slipped into a drugstore by the back door and began dickering with the young drug clerk.

His mission was destined to yield great wealth to many people. It was destined to bring to the South the most far-flung benefit since the Civil War.

For more than an hour, behind the prescription counter, the

old doctor and the clerk talked in low tones. Then the doctor left. He went out to the buggy and brought back a large, old-fashioned kettle, a big wooden paddle (used for stirring the contents of the kettle) and deposited them in the back of the store.

The clerk inspected the kettle, reached into his inside pocket, took out a roll of bills, and handed it over to the doctor. The roll contained exactly $500—the clerk's entire savings!

The doctor handed over a small slip of paper on which was written a secret formula. The words on that small slip of paper were worth a king's ransom! But not to the doctor! Those magic words were needed to start the kettle to boiling, but neither the doctor nor the young clerk knew what fabulous fortunes were destined to flow from that kettle.

The old doctor was glad to sell the outfit for $500. The money would pay off his debts and give him freedom of mind. The clerk was taking a big chance by staking his entire life's savings on a mere scrap of paper and an old kettle! He never dreamed his investment would start a kettle to overflowing with gold that would surpass the miraculous performance of Aladdin's lamp.

What the clerk really purchased was an IDEA!

The old kettle, the wooden paddle and the secret message on a slip of paper were incidental. The strange performance of that kettle began to take place after the new owner mixed with the secret instructions an ingredient of which the doctor knew nothing.

Read this story carefully and give your imagination a test! See if you can discover what it was that the young man added to the secret message that caused the kettle to overflow with gold. Remember as you read that this is not a story from *Arabian Nights*. Here you have a story of facts, stranger than fiction, facts which began in the form of an IDEA.

Let us take a look at the vast fortunes of gold this idea has produced. It has paid, and still pays, huge fortunes to men and women all over the world who distribute the contents of the kettle to millions of people.

The Old Kettle is now one of the world's largest consumers of sugar, thus providing jobs of a permanent nature to thousands of men and women engaged in growing sugar cane, beets, other sugar producing crops and in refining and marketing sugar.

The Old Kettle consumes millions and millions of bottles and cans each year, providing jobs to huge numbers of workers who manufacture those containers.

The Old Kettle gives employment to an army of clerks, stenographers, copywriters and advertising experts throughout the nation. It has brought fame and fortune to scores of artists who have created magnificent pictures and ads describing the product.

The Old Kettle converted a small Southern city into the business capital of the South, where it now benefits, directly or indirectly, every business and practically every resident of the city.

The influence of this idea now benefits every civilized country in the world, pouring out a continuous stream of gold to all who touch it.

Gold from the kettle has built and maintains one of the most prominent universities of the South, where thousands of young people receive the training essential for success.

The Old Kettle has done other marvellous things. All during the Depression, when factories, banks and businesses were folding up and quitting by the thousands, the owner of this Enchanted Kettle went marching on, giving continuous employment to an army of men and women all over the world, and paying out extra portions of gold to those who long ago had faith in the idea.

If the product of that old brass kettle could talk, it would tell thrilling tales of romance in every language. Romances of love, romances of business, romances of professional men and women who are daily being stimulated by it.

I am sure of at least one such romance, for I was a part of it, and it all began not far from the very spot on which the drug clerk purchased the old kettle. It was here that I met my wife, and it was she who first told me of the Enchanted Kettle. It was the product of that kettle we were drinking when I asked her to accept me 'for better or worse.'.

Whoever you are, wherever you may live, whatever occupation you may be engaged in, just remember in the future, every time you see the words 'Coca-Cola', that its vast empire of wealth and influence grew out of a single IDEA, and that the mysterious ingredient which the drug clerk—Asa Candler—mixed with the secret formula was…IMAGINATION! Stop and think of that for a moment.

Remember also that *The 13 Steps to Riches* were the media through which the influence of Coca-Cola has been extended to every city, town, village and crossroads of the world, and that ANY IDEA you may create, which is as sound and meritorious as Coca-Cola, has the possibility of duplicating the stupendous record of this worldwide thirst-quencher.

Truly, thoughts are things, and their scope of operation is the world itself.

WHAT I WOULD DO IF I HAD A MILLION DOLLARS

The following story proves the truth of the old saying, 'Where there's a will, there's a way.' It was told to me by that beloved educator and clergyman, the late Frank W. Gunsaulus, who began his preaching career in the stockyards region of South Chicago.

While Dr Gunsaulus was going through college, he observed many defects in our educational system, defects which he believed he could correct if he were the head of a college. His deepest desire was to become the head of an educational institution in which young men and women would be taught to learn by doing.

He made up his mind to organize a new college in which he could carry out his ideas without being handicapped by orthodox methods of education.

He needed a million dollars to put the project across! Where was he to lay his hands on so large a sum of money? That was the question that absorbed most of this ambitious young preacher's thought.

But he couldn't seem to make any progress.

Every night he took that thought to bed with him. He got up with it in the morning. He took it with him everywhere he went. He turned it over and over in his mind until it became a consuming *obsession* with him. A million dollars is a lot of money. He recognized that fact, but he also recognized the truth that *the only limitation is that which one sets up in one's own mind*.

Being a philosopher as well as a preacher, Dr Gunsaulus recognized, as do all who succeed in life, that DEFINITENESS OF PURPOSE is the starting point from which one must begin. He recognized, too, that definiteness of purpose takes on animation, life and power when backed by a BURNING DESIRE to translate that purpose into its material equivalent.

He knew all these great truths, yet he did not know where or how to lay his hands on a million dollars. The natural procedure would have been to give up and quit by saying, 'Ah well, my idea is a good one, but I cannot do anything with it because I never can procure the necessary million dollars.' That is exactly what the majority of people would have said, but it is not what Dr Gunsaulus said. What he said and what he did are so important that I now introduce him and let him speak for himself.

'One Saturday afternoon I sat in my room thinking of ways and means of raising the money to carry out my plans. For nearly two years I had been thinking, but I *had done nothing but think!*

'The time had come for ACTION!

'I made up my mind, then and there, that I would get the necessary million dollars within a week. How? I was not concerned about that. The thing of importance was the *decision* to get the money within a specified time, and I want to tell you that the moment I reached a definite decision to get the money within a specified time, a strange feeling of assurance came over me such as I had never before experienced. Something inside me seemed to say, "Why didn't you reach that decision a long time ago? The money was waiting for you all the time!"

'Things began to happen in a hurry. I called the newspapers and announced I would preach a sermon the following morning entitled, "What I Would Do If I Had a Million Dollars".

'I went to work on the sermon immediately, but I must tell you frankly the task was not difficult because I had been preparing that sermon for almost two years. The spirit back of it was a part of me!

'Long before midnight I had finished writing the sermon. I went to bed and slept with a feeling of confidence, for *I could see myself already in possession of the million dollars.*

'Next morning, I arose early, went into the bathroom, read

the sermon, then knelt on my knees and asked that my sermon might come to the attention of someone who would supply the needed money.

'While I was praying, I again had that feeling of assurance that the money would be forthcoming. In my excitement, I walked out without my sermon and did not discover the oversight until I was in my pulpit and about ready to begin delivering it.

'It was too late to go back for my notes, and what a blessing that I couldn't go back! Instead, my own subconscious mind yielded the material I needed. When I arose to begin my sermon, I closed my eyes, and spoke with all my heart and soul of my dreams. I not only talked to my audience, but I fancy I talked also to God. I told what I would do with a million dollars if that amount were placed in my hands. I described the plan I had in mind for organizing a great educational institution where young people would learn to do practical things and at the same time develop their minds.

'When I had finished and sat down, a man slowly arose from his seat, about three rows from the rear, and made his way toward the pulpit. I wondered what he was going to do. He came into the pulpit, extended his hand, and said, "Reverend, I liked your sermon. I believe you can do everything you said you would if you had a million dollars. To prove that I believe in you and your sermon, if you will come to my office tomorrow morning, I will give you the million dollars. My name is Phillip D. Armour."

Young Gunsaulus went to Mr. Armour's office and the million dollars was presented to him. With the money he founded the Armour Institute of Technology.

That is more money than the majority of preachers ever see in an entire lifetime, yet the thought impulse back of the money was created in the young preacher's mind in a fraction of a minute. The necessary million dollars came as a result of an idea. Back of the idea was a DESIRE which young Gunsaulus had been nursing in his mind for almost two years.

Observe this important fact—HE GOT THE MONEY WITHIN 36 HOURS AFTER HE REACHED A DEFINITE DECISION IN HIS OWN MIND TO GET IT—AND DECIDED UPON A DEFINITE PLAN FOR GETTING IT!

There was nothing new or unique about young Gunsaulus' vague thinking about a million dollars and weakly hoping for it. Others before him, and many since his time, have had similar thoughts. But there was something unique and different about the decision he reached on that memorable Saturday, when he put vagueness into the background and said definitely, 'I WILL get that money within a week!'

God seems to throw Himself on the side of people who know exactly what they want, if they are determined to get JUST THAT!

Moreover, the principle through which Dr Gunsaulus got his million dollars is still alive! It is available to you! This universal law is as workable today as it was when the young preacher made use of it so successfully.

Observe that Asa Candler and Dr Frank Gunsaulus had one characteristic in common. Both knew the astounding truth that IDEAS CAN BE TRANSMUTED INTO CASH THROUGH THE POWER OF **DEFINITE PURPOSE, PLUS DEFINITE PLANS.**

If you are one of those who believe that hard work and honesty alone will bring riches, perish the thought! It is not true! Riches, when they come in huge quantities, are never the result of HARD work! Riches come, if they come at all, in response to definite demands, based upon the application of definite principles, and not by chance or luck.

Generally speaking, an idea is an impulse of thought that impels action by an appeal to the imagination. All master salespeople know that ideas can be sold where merchandise cannot. Ordinary salespeople do *not* know this —that is why they are ordinary.

A publisher of books which sell for a few dollars made a discovery that should be worth much to publishers generally. He learned that many people buy titles and not contents of books. By merely changing the name of one book that was not moving, his sales on that book jumped upward more than a million copies. The inside of the book was not changed in any way. He merely ripped off the cover bearing the title that did not sell, and put on a new cover with a title that had 'box office' value.

That, as simple as it may seem, was an IDEA! It was IMAGINATION at work.

There is no standard price on ideas. Creators of ideas make their own price and, if they are smart, get it.

The movie industry created a whole flock of millionaires. Most of them were individuals who couldn't create ideas— BUT—they had the imagination to recognize ideas when they saw them.

The story of practically every great fortune starts with the day when a creator of ideas and a seller of ideas get together and work in harmony. Carnegie surrounded himself with people who could do all that he could not do—people who created ideas and people who put ideas into operation— and by so doing made himself and the others fabulously rich.

Millions of people go through life hoping for favourable breaks. Perhaps a favourable break can get one an opportunity, but the safest plan is not to depend upon luck. It was a favourable 'break' that gave me the biggest opportunity of my life—*but*—25 years of *determined effort* had to be devoted to that opportunity before it became an asset.

The break consisted of my good fortune in meeting and gaining the cooperation of Andrew Carnegie. On that occasion, Carnegie planted in my mind the idea of organizing the principles of achievement into a philosophy of success. Thousands of people have profited by the discoveries made in the twenty-five years of research, and numerous fortunes have been accumulated through the application of the philosophy. The beginning was simple. It was an IDEA which anyone might have developed.

The favourable break came through Andrew Carnegie, but what about the DETERMINATION, DEFINITENESS OF PURPOSE, the DESIRE TO ATTAIN THE GOAL and the PERSISTENT EFFORT OF TWENTY-FIVE YEARS? It was no ordinary DESIRE that survived disappointment, discouragement, temporary defeat, criticism and the constant reminding of 'waste of time'. It was a BURNING DESIRE! An OBSESSION!

When the idea was first planted in my mind by Mr Carnegie, it was coaxed, nursed and enticed to *remain alive*. Gradually, the idea became a giant, under its own power, and it coaxed, nursed and drove me. Ideas are like that. First you give life and action and guidance to ideas, then they take on power of their own and sweep aside all opposition.

Ideas are intangible forces, but they have more power than the physical brains that give birth to them. They have the power to live on, after the brain that creates them has returned to dust. For example, take the power of Christianity. That began with a simple idea. Its chief tenet was, 'Do unto others as you would have others do unto you.' Christ has gone back to the source from whence He came, but His IDEA goes marching on. Some day, it may come fully into its own. Then it will have fulfilled Christ's deepest DESIRE. The IDEA has been developing only some two thousand years. Give it time!

POINTS TO REMEMBER

1. Ideas in your mind that do not have enthusiasm, or faith will seldom produce any action.
2. Rearranging old ideas and old concepts can be very profitable.
3. The principles that guarantee to help you achieve your ambition.

6

FAILURE

An all-wise Providence has arranged the affairs of mankind so that every person who comes into the age of reason must bear the cross of FAILURE in one form or another.

Hundreds of millions of people living on this earth today find it necessary to struggle under the burden of poverty in order to enjoy the three bare necessities of life, a place to sleep, something to eat and clothes to wear.

Carrying the cross of POVERTY is no joke!

But, it seems significant that the greatest and most successful men and women who ever lived found it necessary to carry this cross before they 'arrived'.

FAILURE is generally accepted as a curse. But few people ever understand that failure is a curse only when it is accepted as such. But few ever learn the truth that FAILURE is seldom permanent.

Go back over your own experiences for a few years and you will see that your failures generally turned out to be blessings in disguise. Failure teaches men lessons which they would never learn without it. Moreover, it teaches in a language that is universal. Among the great lessons taught by failure is that of HUMILITY.

No man may become great without feeling himself

humble and insignificant when compared to the world about him and the stars above him and the harmony with which Nature does her work.

For every rich man's son who becomes a useful, constructive worker in behalf of humanity, there are ninety-nine others rendering useful service who come up through POVERTY and misery. This seems more than a coincidence!

Most people who believe themselves to be failures are not failures at all. Most conditions which people look upon as failure are nothing more than temporary defeat.

If you pity yourself and feel that you are a failure, think how much worse off you would be if you had to change places with others who have real cause for complaint.

In the city of Chicago lives a beautiful young woman. Her eyes are a light blue. Her complexion is extremely fair. She has a sweet charming voice. She is educated and cultured. Three days after graduating in one of the colleges of the East she discovered that she had negro blood in her veins.

The man to whom she was engaged refused to marry her. The negroes do not want her and the whites will not associate with her. During the remainder of her life she must bear the brand of permanent FAILURE.

Remember, this is PERMANENT failure!

As this essay is being written news comes of a beautiful girl baby who was born to an unwed girl and taken into an orphanage, there to be brought up mechanically, without ever knowing the influence of a mother's love. All through life this unfortunate child must bear the brunt of another's mistake which can never be corrected.

How fortunate are YOU, no matter what may be your imaginary failures, that you are not this child.

If you have a strong body and a sound mind you have

much for which you ought to be thankful. Millions of people all about you have no such blessings.

Do not use the word FAILURE carelessly.

Remember, carrying a burdensome cross temporarily is not FAILURE. If you have the real seed of success within you, a little adversity and temporary defeat will only serve to nurture that seed and cause it to burst forth into maturity.

There is no FAILURE. That which looks to be failure is usually nothing but temporary defeat. Make sure that you do not accept it as PERMANENT!

POINTS TO REMEMBER

1. Everyone must bear the cross of failure.
2. Most people who believe themselves to be failures are not failures at all.
3. If you have a strong body and a sound mind you have much for which you ought to be thankful.

7

YOU'VE GOT A PROBLEM? THAT'S GOOD!

So you've got a problem? That's good! Why? Because repeated victories over your problems are the rungs on your ladder of success. With each victory you grow in wisdom, stature and experience. You become a better, bigger, more successful person each time you meet a problem and tackle and conquer it with PMA.

Stop and think about it for a moment. Do you know of a single instance where any real achievement was made in your life, or in the life of any person in history, that was not due to a problem with which the individual was faced?

Everyone has problems. This is because you and everything in the universe are in a constant process of change. Change is an inexorable natural law. What is important to you is that your success or failure to meet the challenges of change are dependent upon your mental attitude.

You can direct your thoughts and control your emotions, and thus regulate your attitude. You can choose whether your attitude will be positive or negative. You can decide whether you will affect, use, control or harmonize with the changes in yourself and your environment. You can ordain your destiny.

When you meet the challenges of change with PMA, you can intelligently solve each problem with which you are confronted.

How do you meet a problem with PMA? If you know and believe the first principal element of a positive mental attitude: God is always a good God—then you can effectively use the following formula and meet your problems:

ASKING THE RIGHT QUESTIONS WHEN STUCK WITH A PROBLEM

When you are faced with a problem that needs a solution, regardless of how perplexing it may be:

1. Ask for Divine Guidance. Ask for help in finding the right solution.
2. Engage in thinking time for the purpose of solving your problems. Remember that every adversity has the seed of an equivalent or greater benefit for those who have PMA.
3. State the problem. Analyse and define it.
4. State *to yourself* enthusiastically, 'That's good!'
5. Ask yourself some specific questions, such as:
    a. What's good about it?
    b. How can I turn this adversity into a seed of equivalent or greater benefit; or how can I turn this liability into a greater asset?
6. Keep searching for answers to these questions until you find at least one answer that *can work*.

Now the problems that will confront you will, broadly speaking, be of three kinds: personal problems—emotional, financial, mental, moral, physical; family problems; and business or professional problems.

Another force with which every human being has to contend, and which, if not met with PMA, can cause physical, moral and mental destruction is the power of sex. Sex presents the greatest challenge of change! Each human being has the power to choose for himself whether he will use the tremendous power of sex for good or for evil. Each human being must contend with the problems that will arise in his life because of sex.

You can transmute sex into virtue or vice. One of God's greatest gifts to mankind is the power to procreate a human being. Sex is the means of procreation. It is power! Like all power, it can be used for good or for evil.

Sex is a physical function of the body under the control of the subconscious and conscious mind. It is inherited. The physical sex organs, works of God, like all His creations, are good. The little difference that makes the big difference between the power of sex being a virtue or a vice is *mental attitude*.

The inherent emotion of sex is one of the most powerful forces of the subconscious mind. The effects of its motivating power can be observed long before adolescence. This power blends with and intensifies the driving force of all other emotions.

When it is in conflict with the will of the conscious mind, the power of imagination, as it affects the emotion of sex, has a tendency to win unless the conscious mind uses its power to affect, use, control or harmonize with the powers of the subconscious. You have the power to choose. Choose wisely—with PMA. Transmute sex into virtue! Thus you will win over one of the greatest problems you will ever have to face in your personal life. And you will be physically, mentally and morally better.

THE SEVEN HEAVENLY VIRTUES

And what are the seven virtues? *Virtue* is moral practice or action, moral excellence; rectitude; valour; chastity. The seven virtues are: *prudence, fortitude, temperance, justice, faith, hope and charity.*

1. *Prudence*—the ability to govern and discipline one's self by the exercise of reason.
2. *Fortitude*—strength of mind that enables a person to encounter danger or bear pain or adversity with courage. It is the possession of the stamina essential to face that which repels or frightens one, or to put up with the hardships of a task imposed. It implies triumph. Synonyms are grit, backbone, pluck and guts.
3. *Temperance*—habitual moderation in the indulgence of the appetites and passions.
4. *Justice*—the principle or ideal of just dealing or right action; also conformity to this principle or ideal; integrity.
5. *Faith*—trust in God.
6. *Hope*—the desire with expectation of obtaining what is desired, or belief that it is obtainable.
7. *Charity*—the act of loving all men as brothers because they are sons of God. It stresses benevolence and goodwill in giving and in the broad understanding of others with kindly tolerance.

How can you transmute the power of sex into the good and the beautiful? A crystal-clear answer can be found by you if you search for it as you read and study this entire book. Results will be achieved when you relate and assimilate the principles into your own life.

But one must gain knowledge for himself. The following suggestions may be helpful as you search for your answer while reading:

1. Keep your mind on the things you want and off the things you don't want. This means that you keep your mind on immediate, intermediate and distant desirable objectives. The instinct of sex in the subconscious mind will be patient if it has hope that you will fulfil life's mission. The boy or girl who is truly in love and plans to marry will not have the sex problems he or she might otherwise have.
2. If there were more and often earlier marriages, there would be fewer sex problems. Life's mission to procreate is fulfilled in marriage; however, marry for love beyond the sex instinct.
3. Lead a well-balanced, four-square life.
4. Work long hours at a labour of love. It will keep you busy, occupy your thoughts, and use up surplus energy.
5. Develop a Magnificent Obsession.
6. Relate and assimilate into your own life the concepts 'You Can Change Your World!' and 'Learn to See'.
7. Select an environment that will develop you best toward your objectives.
8. Choose the self-motivators for self-suggestion that you believe will help you. Memorize them. Make them a part of yourself so that in times of need they will flash from your subconscious mind to your conscious mind as autosuggestion.

Not all the problems of one's personal life, however, are of so deep and penetrating a nature. Many times all that it takes to meet an immediate problem is quick thinking, adaptability and taking a second look at the situation which is causing the problem. It often takes only one idea, followed by action, to turn failure into success.

A man who seizes upon his problems as opportunities in disguise and scrutinizes them for the good element that is going to be there is the man who understands the very core of PMA. The man who develops an idea that can work and follows it with action will turn failure into success.

POINTS TO REMEMBER

1. You become a better, bigger, more successful person each time you meet a problem and tackle and conquer it.
2. Select an environment that will develop you best toward your objectives.
3. Your success or failure to meet the challenges of change are dependent upon your mental attitude.

8

HOW TO OUTWIT THE GHOSTS OF FEAR

BEFORE YOU CAN put any portion of *The Think and Grow Rich Philosophy* into successful use, your mind must be prepared to receive it. The preparation is not difficult. It begins with study, analysis and an understanding of three enemies which you shall have to clear out.

These are INDECISION, DOUBT and FEAR!

The Sixth Sense will never function while these three negatives or any one of them remains in your mind. The members of this unholy trio are closely tied. Where one is found the other two are close at hand.

INDECISION is the seedling of FEAR! And remember this as you read. Indecision crystallizes DOUBT. The two blend and become FEAR! This blending process often is slow. This is one reason why these three enemies are so dangerous. They germinate and grow *without their presence being observed.*

The remainder of this chapter describes an end which must be attained before *The Think and Grow Rich Philosophy*, as a whole, can be put into practical use. It also analyses a condition which has reduced large numbers of people to poverty, and it states a truth which must be understood by all who would accumulate riches, whether measured in terms of money or a state of mind of far greater value than money.

Let us now turn the spotlight on the cause and the cure of the Six Basic Fears. Before we can master an enemy, we must know its name, its habits and its place of abode. As you read, analyse yourself carefully and determine which, if any, of the six common fears have attached themselves to you. Do not be deceived by the habits of these subtle enemies. Sometimes they remain hidden in the subconscious mind, where they are difficult to locate and still more difficult to eradicate.

THE SIX BASIC FEARS

There are Six Basic Fears, with some combination of which every human being suffers at one time or another. Most people are fortunate if they do not suffer from the entire six. Named in the order of their most common appearance, they are:

The fear of POVERTY (at the heart of most people's worries)
The fear of CRITICISM
The fear of ILL HEALTH
The fear of LOSS OF LOVE OF SOMEONE
The fear of OLD AGE
The fear of DEATH

All other fears are of minor importance. They can be grouped under these six headings.

The prevalence of these fears, as a curse to the world, runs in cycles. For almost six years, while the Depression was on, we floundered in the cycle of FEAR OF POVERTY. During World War I we were in the cycle of FEAR OF DEATH. Just following the war, we were in the cycle of FEAR OF ILL

HEALTH, as evidenced by the epidemic of disease which spread all over the world.

Fears are nothing more than states of mind. As has been demonstrated repeatedly in the chapters of this book, one's state of mind is subject to control and direction.

An individual can create nothing which he or she does not first *conceive* in the form of an impulse of thought. Following this statement comes another of still greater importance, namely, that THOUGHT IMPULSES BEGIN IMMEDIATELY TO TRANSLATE THEMSELVES INTO THEIR PHYSICAL EQUIVALENT, WHETHER THOSE THOUGHTS ARE VOLUNTARY OR INVOLUNTARY. Thought impulses which are picked up by mere chance from sources outside one's own mind (thoughts created in other minds) may determine one's financial, business, professional or social destiny just as surely as do the thought impulses which one creates by intent and design.

We are here laying the foundation for the presentation of a fact of great importance to the person who does not understand why some people appear to be lucky while others of equal or greater ability, training, experience and intellectual capacity seem destined to misfortune. This fact may be explained by the statement that *all human beings have the ability to completely control their own mind*, and with this control, obviously, all individuals can open their minds to the 'tramp' thought impulses which derive from the brains of others, or else can close the doors tightly and admit only thought impulses of their own choice.

Nature has endowed human beings with absolute control over only one thing—and that is THOUGHT. This fact—coupled with the additional fact that everything that human beings create begins in the form of a *thought*, an IDEA—leads one very near to the principle by which FEAR may be mastered.

If it is true that ALL THOUGHT HAS A TENDENCY TO CLOTHE ITSELF IN ITS PHYSICAL EQUIVALENT (and this is true beyond any doubt), it is equally true that thought impulses of fear and poverty cannot be translated into terms of courage and financial gain.

The people of America began to think of poverty following the Wall Street crash of 1929. Slowly but surely, that mass thought was crystallized into its physical equivalent, which was known as a depression. This had to happen. It is in conformity with the laws of Nature.

THE FEAR OF POVERTY

There can be no compromise between POVERTY and RICHES! The roads that lead to poverty and riches travel in opposite directions. If you want riches, you must refuse to accept any circumstance that leads toward poverty. (The word 'riches' is here used in its broadest sense, meaning financial, spiritual, mental and material estates). The starting point of the path that leads to riches is DESIRE. You received full instructions for the proper use of DESIRE. Now in this concluding discussion on FEAR you will receive complete instructions for preparing your mind to make practical use of DESIRE.

Here then is the place to give yourself a challenge which will definitely determine how much of this philosophy you have absorbed so far. Here is the point at which you can turn prophet and foretell accurately what the future holds in store for you. If, after reading what follows, you are willing to accept poverty, you may as well make up your mind to receive poverty. This is one decision you cannot avoid.

If you demand riches, determine what form of riches and

how much will be required to satisfy you. You should now know the road that leads to riches. You have been given a road map which, if followed, will keep you on that road. If you neglect to make the start, or stop before you arrive, no one will be to blame but YOU. The responsibility is yours. No alibi will save you from accepting this responsibility. If you now fail or refuse to demand riches of life, it will be because of one thing—the only thing you can truly control—a STATE OF MIND. And a state of mind is something that one *assumes*. It cannot be purchased. It must be *created*.

Fear of poverty is a state of mind, nothing else! But it is sufficient to destroy one's chances of achievement in any undertaking, a truth which becomes painfully evident during any time of economic difficulty and uncertainty.

Fear of poverty paralyses the faculty of reason, destroys the faculty of imagination, kills self-reliance, undermines enthusiasm, discourages initiative, leads to uncertainty of purpose, encourages procrastination, wipes out enthusiasm and makes self-control impossible. It takes the charm from one's personality, destroys the possibility of accurate thinking, diverts concentration of effort, kills persistence, turns willpower into nothingness, destroys ambition, beclouds memory and invites failure in every conceivable form. It kills love and assassinates the finer emotions of the heart, discourages friendship, invites disaster in a hundred forms, leads to sleeplessness, misery and unhappiness—and all this despite the obvious truth that we live in a world of overabundance of everything the heart could desire, with nothing standing between us and our desires except *lack of a definite purpose and the plans that derive from it.*

The Fear of Poverty is without doubt the most destructive of the Six Basic Fears. It has been placed at the head of the list because it is the most difficult fear to master. Considerable courage is required to state the truth about the origin of this fear, and still greater courage to accept the truth after it has been stated. The fear of poverty grew out of human beings' inherited tendency to PREY UPON OTHERS ECONOMICALLY. Nearly all animals are motivated by instinct, but their capacity to think is limited; therefore, they prey upon one another physically. Human beings, with their superior sense of intuition and the capacity to think and to reason, do not eat other human beings bodily—they get more satisfaction out of 'eating' them FINANCIALLY. Human beings, by nature, are so avaricious that every conceivable law has been passed to safeguard them from each other.

Of all the ages of the world of which we know anything, the age in which we live seems to be one that is most characterized by 'moneymadness'. People are almost considered less than the dust of the earth unless they can display a fat bank account. But if they have money— NEVER MIND HOW THEY ACQUIRED IT—they are 'royalty' or 'big shots'. They seem above the law, they rule in politics, they dominate in business and the whole world about them bows in respect when they pass.

Nothing brings a person so much suffering and humility as POVERTY! Only those who have experienced poverty understand the full meaning of this.

It is no wonder that people fear poverty. Through a long line of inherited experiences, people have learned, for sure, that some individuals cannot be trusted where matters of money and earthly possessions are concerned. This is a stinging, but true indictment.

The majority of marriages continue to be motivated by the wealth possessed by one or both of the contracting parties. It is no wonder, therefore, that the divorce courts stay busy. So eager are people to possess wealth that they will acquire it in whatever manner they can—through legal methods if possible, through other methods if necessary or expedient.

Self-analysis may disclose weaknesses which one does not like to acknowledge. This form of examination is essential for all who demand of life more than mediocrity and poverty. Remember, as you check yourself point by point, that you are both the court and the jury, the prosecuting attorney and the attorney for the defence, the plaintiff and the defendant—and it is YOU who are on trial. Face the facts squarely. Ask yourself definite questions and demand direct replies. When your examination is over, you will know more about yourself. If you do not feel that you can be an impartial judge in this self-examination, call upon someone who knows you well to serve as judge while you cross-examine yourself. You are after the truth. Get it, no matter at what cost even though it may temporarily embarrass you!

The majority of people, if asked what they fear most, would reply, 'I fear nothing.' The reply would be inaccurate because few people realize that they are bound, handicapped, and whipped spiritually and physically by some form of fear. So subtle and deeply seated is the emotion of fear that one may go through life burdened with it, never recognizing its presence. Only a courageous analysis will disclose the presence of this universal enemy. When you begin such an analysis, search deeply into your character. Here is a list of the symptoms for which you should look:

SYMPTOMS OF THE FEAR OF POVERTY

INDIFFERENCE. Commonly expressed through lack of ambition; willingness to tolerate poverty; acceptance of whatever compensation life may offer without protest; mental and physical laziness; lack of initiative, imagination, enthusiasm and self-control

INDECISION. The habit of permitting others to do one's thinking. Staying on the fence.

DOUBT. Generally expressed through alibis and excuses designed to cover up, explain away or apologize for one's failures, sometimes expressed in the form of envy of those who are successful or by criticism of them.

WORRY. Usually expressed by finding fault with others, a tendency to spend beyond one's income, neglect of personal appearance, scowling and frowning; intemperance in the use of alcoholic, sometimes through the use of narcotics; nervousness, lack of poise, self-consciousness and lack of self-reliance.

OVER-CAUTION. The habit of looking for the negative side of every circumstance, thinking and talking of possible failure instead of concentrating upon the means of succeeding. Knowing all the roads to disaster, but never searching for the plans to avoid failure. Waiting for the 'right time' to begin putting ideas and plans into action, until the waiting becomes a permanent habit. Remembering those who have failed, and forgetting those who have succeeded. Seeing the hole in the doughnut, but overlooking the doughnut. Pessimism, leading to indigestion, poor elimination, autointoxication, bad breath and bad disposition.

PROCRASTINATION. The habit of putting off until tomorrow that which should have been done last year. Spending enough time in creating alibis and excuses to have done the job. This symptom is closely related to over-caution, doubt and worry. Refusal to accept responsibility when it can be avoided. Willingness to compromise rather than put up a stiff fight. Compromising with difficulties instead of harnessing and using them as steppingstones to advancement. Bargaining with life for a penny, instead of demanding prosperity, opulence, riches, contentment and happiness. Planning what to do IF AND WHEN OVERTAKEN BY FAILURE, INSTEAD OF BURNING ALL BRIDGES AND MAKING RETREAT IMPOSSIBLE. Weakness of, and often total lack of, self-confidence, definiteness of purpose, self-control, initiative, enthusiasm, ambition, thrift and sound reasoning ability. EXPECTING POVERTY INSTEAD OF DEMANDING RICHES. Association with those who accept poverty instead of seeking the company of those who demand and receive riches.

MONEY TALKS!

Some will ask, 'Why did you write a book about money? Why measure riches in dollars alone?' Some will believe, and rightly so, that there are other forms of riches more desirable than money. Yes, there are riches which cannot be measured in terms of dollars, but there are millions of people who will say, 'Give me all the money I need, and I will find everything else I want.'

The major reason I wrote this book on how to get money is the fact that the world has but lately passed through an experience that left millions of men and women paralysed with the FEAR OF POVERTY. What this sort of fear does to one was well described by Westbrook Pegler in the *New York World-Telegram*:

> Money is only clam shells or metal discs or scraps of paper, and there are treasures of the heart and soul

which money cannot buy, but most people, being broke, are unable to keep this in mind and sustain their spirits. When a man is down and out and on the street, unable to get any job at all, something happens to his spirit which can be observed in the droop of his shoulders, the set of his hat, his walk and his gaze. He cannot escape a feeling of inferiority among people with regular employment, even though he knows they are definitely not his equals in character, intelligence or ability.

These people—even his friends—feel, on the other hand, a sense of superiority and regard him, perhaps unconsciously, as a casualty. He may borrow for a time, but not enough to carry on in his accustomed way, and he cannot continue to borrow very long. But borrowing in itself, when a man is borrowing merely to live, is a depressing experience, and the money lacks the power of earned money to revive his spirits. Of course, none of this applies to bums or habitual ne'er-do-wells, but only to men of normal ambitions and self-respect.

Women in the same predicament must be different. We somehow do not think of women at all in considering the down-and-outers. They are...not recognizable in crowds by the same plain signs which identify busted men. Of course, I do not mean the shuffling hags of the city streets who are the opposite number of the confirmed male bums. I mean reasonably young, decent and intelligent women. There must be many of them, but their despair is not apparent...

When a man is down and out, he has time on his hands for brooding. He may travel miles to see a man about a job and discover that the job is filled or that it is one of those jobs with no base pay but only a commission on the sale of some useless knickknack which nobody would buy... Turning that down, he finds himself back on the street with nowhere to go but just anywhere. So he walks and walks. He gazes into store windows at luxuries which are not for him, and feels inferior and gives way to people who stop to look with an active interest. He wanders into the railroad station or puts himself down in the library to ease his legs and soak up a little heat, but that isn't looking for a job, so he gets going again. He may not know it, but his aimlessness would give him away even if the very lines of his figure did not. He may be well dressed in the clothes left over from the days when he had a steady job, but the clothes cannot disguise the droop...

He sees thousands of other people, bookkeepers or clerks or chemists...busy at their work and envies them from the bottom of his soul. They have their independence, their self-respect and manhood, and he simply cannot convince himself that he is a good man, too, though he argue it out and arrive at a favourable verdict hour after hour.

It is just money which makes this difference in him. With a little money he would be himself again.

THE FEAR OF CRITICISM

Just how humanity originally came by this fear, no one can state definitely, but one thing is certain—people have it in a highly developed form. I am inclined to attribute the basic fear of criticism to that part of inherited human nature which prompts people not only to take away the goods and wares of others, but to justify their action by CRITICISM of their victims' character. It is a well-known fact that thieves will criticize those from whom they steal and that politicians seek office not by displaying their own virtues and qualifications, but by attempting to besmirch their opponents.

The Fear of Criticism takes on many forms, the majority of which are petty and trivial. The astute manufacturers of clothing have not been slow to capitalize on this basic fear, with which all humanity has been cursed. Every season the styles in many articles of wearing apparel change. Who establishes the styles? Certainly not the purchaser of clothing, but the manufacturers. Why do they change the styles so often? The answer is obvious. They change the styles so they can sell more clothes.

For the same reason the manufacturers of automobiles (with a few rare and very sensible exceptions) change styles of models every season. No one wants to drive an automobile which is not of the latest style, although the older model may actually be the better car.

We have been describing the manner in which people behave under the influence of the Fear of Criticism as applied to the small and petty things of life. Let us now examine human behaviour when this fear affects people in connection with the more important events of human relationship. Take, for example, practically any person who has reached the age of mental maturity (from thirty to forty years of age, as a general average), and if you could read the secret thoughts of his or her mind, you would find a very decided disbelief in most of the fables taught by the majority of the dogmatists and theologians a few decades back.

Not often, however, will you find an individual who has the courage to openly state his or her belief on this subject. Most people will, if pressed far enough, tell a lie rather than admit that they do not believe all of the stories associated with a religion, particularly if their religion (or sect) is one of those which are rigidly dogmatic and intolerant of questioning.

Why does the average person, even in this day of enlightenment, shy away from denying his or her belief in those aspects of religious dogma that are almost surely 'fabulous', or fable-like? The answer is 'the Fear of Criticism'. Men and women have been burned at the stake for daring to express their disbelief in ghosts. It is no wonder we have inherited a consciousness which makes us fear criticism. The time was, and not so far in the past, when criticism carried severe punishments—and still does in many countries.

The Fear of Criticism robs people of their initiative, destroys their power of imagination, limits their individuality, takes away their self-reliance and does them damage in a hundred other ways. Parents often do their children irreparable injury by criticizing them. The mother of one of my boyhood chums used to punish him with a switch almost daily, always completing the job with the statement, 'You'll land in the penitentiary before you are 20.' He was sent to a reformatory at the age of 17.

Criticism is the one form of 'service' of which everyone has too much. Everyone has a stock of it which is handed out gratis, whether asked for or not. One's nearest relatives often are the worst offenders. It should be recognized as a crime (in reality, it is a crime of the worst nature) for any parent to create an inferiority complex in the mind of a child through unnecessary criticism. Employers who understand human nature get the best there is in their employees not by criticism, but by constructive suggestion. Parents may accomplish the same results with their children. Criticism will plant FEAR in the human heart, or resentment, but it will not build love or affection.

SYMPTOMS OF THE FEAR OF CRITICISM

This fear is almost as universal as the Fear of Poverty, and its effects are just as fatal to personal achievement, mainly because this fear destroys initiative and discourages the use of imagination. The major symptoms of the fear are:

SELF-CONSCIOUSNESS. Generally expressed through nervousness, timidity in conversation and in meeting strangers, awkward movement of the hands and limbs, shifting of the eyes. LACK OF POISE. Expressed through lack of voice control, nervousness in the presence of others, poor posture of body, poor memory.

WEAK PERSONALITY. Lacking in firmness of decision, personal charm and ability to express opinions definitely. The habit of sidestepping issues instead of meeting them squarely. Agreeing with others without careful examination of their opinions.

INFERIORITY COMPLEX. The habit of expressing self-approval by word of mouth and by actions, as a means of covering up a feeling of inferiority. Using big words to impress others (often without knowing the real meaning of the words). Imitating others in dress, speech and manners. Boasting of imaginary achievements. This sometimes gives a surface appearance of a feeling of superiority.

EXTRAVAGANCE. The habit of trying to keep up with the Jones, spending beyond one's income.

LACK OF INITIATIVE. Failure to embrace opportunities for self-advancement, fear to express opinions, lack of confidence in one's own ideas, giving evasive answers to questions asked by superiors, hesitancy of manner and speech, deceit in both words and deeds.

LACK OF AMBITION. Mental and physical laziness, lack of self-assertion, slowness in reaching decisions, tendency to be easily influenced by others, the habit of criticizing others behind their backs and flattering them to their faces, the habit of accepting defeat without protest, quitting an undertaking when opposed by others, being suspicious of other people without cause, lacking tact in manner and speech, unwillingness to accept the blame for mistakes.

THE FEAR OF ILL HEALTH

This fear may be traced to both physical and social heredity. As to its origin, it is closely associated with the causes of the Fear of Old Age and the Fear of Death because it leads us closely to the border of terrible worlds of which we know not, but concerning which we have been taught some discomforting stories. Also, certain unethical people engaged in the business of 'selling health' have had not a little to do with keeping alive the Fear of Ill Health.

In the main, we fear ill health because of the terrible pictures which have been planted in our mind of what may happen if death should overtake us. We also fear it because of the economic toll which it may claim.

A reputable physician estimated that 75 per cent of all people who visit physicians for professional service suffer from hypochondria (imaginary illness). It has been shown most convincingly that the fear of disease, even where there is not the slightest cause for fear, often produces the physical symptoms of the disease feared.

Powerful and mighty is the human mind! It builds or it destroys.

Playing upon this common weakness of Fear of Ill Health, dispensers of patent medicines have reaped fortunes. This form of imposition upon credulous humanity became so prevalent some years ago that *Colliers' Weekly Magazine* conducted a bitter campaign against some of the worst offenders in the patent medicine business.

Through a series of experiments conducted some years ago, it was demonstrated that people can be made ill by suggestion alone. We conducted this experiment by causing three acquaintances to visit the 'victims'. Each visitor asked the question, 'What ails you? You look terribly ill.' The first questioner usually provoked a grin and a nonchalant, 'Oh, nothing, I'm all right,' from the victim. The second questioner usually was answered with the statement, 'I don't know exactly, but I do feel badly.' The third questioner was usually met with the frank admission that the victim was actually feeling ill. Try this on acquaintances if you doubt that it will make them uncomfortable, but do not carry the experiment too far because some people may actually develop serious physical symptoms in response to suggestion. (There is a certain religious sect whose members take vengeance upon their enemies by the 'hexing' method. They call it placing a spell on the victim, and there are reliable reports that some individuals have actually died after being hexed.)

There is overwhelming evidence that disease sometimes begins in the form of negative thought impulse. Such an impulse may be passed from one mind to another, by suggestion, or created by an individual in his or her own mind.

A man who was blessed with more wisdom than this incident might indicate, once said, 'When anyone asks me how

I feel, I always want to answer by knocking him down.'

Physicians sometimes send patients into new climates for their health because a change of mental attitude is necessary. The seed of the Fear of Ill Health lives in every human mind. Worry, fear, discouragement and disappointment in love and business affairs cause this seed to germinate and grow. Every form of negative thinking may cause ill health.

Disappointments in business and in love stand at the head of the list of causes of the Fear of Ill Health. A young man suffered a devastating disappointment in love which eventually resulted in his being hospitalized. For months he suffered a debilitating depression. A psychotherapist was called in. The psychotherapist changed nurses, placing the patient under the care of a *very charming young woman* who began (by prearrangement with the therapist) to coddle him and shower him with affection beginning the first day of her arrival on the job. Within three weeks the patient was discharged from the hospital, still suffering, but with an entirely different malady. HE WAS IN LOVE AGAIN. The remedy was a hoax, but the patient and the nurse were later married. Both are in good health at the time of this writing.

SYMPTOMS OF THE FEAR OF ILL HEALTH

The symptoms of this almost universal fear are:

INAPPROPRIATE AUTOSUGGESTION. The habit of the negative use of self-suggestion by looking for and expecting to find the symptoms of all kinds of disease. 'Enjoying' imaginary illness and speaking of it as being real. The habit of trying all fads and 'isms' recommended by others as having therapeutic value. Dwelling on the details of operations, accidents and other forms of illness. Experimenting with diets, physical exercises and reducing schemes without professional guidance. Over-reliance or experimentation with home remedies, patent medicine and quack remedies.

HYPOCHONDRIA. The habit of talking about illness, concentrating the mind upon disease and expecting its appearance until a nervous condition occurs. Nothing that comes in bottles can cure this condition. It is brought on by negative thinking and nothing but positive thought can effect a cure. Hypochondria (a medical term for imaginary disease) is said to do as much damage on occasion as the disease one fears might do. Most so-called cases of nerves come from imaginary illness.

LACK OF EXERCISE. Fear of ill health often interferes with proper physical exercise and results in one's being overweight by causing one to avoid outdoor life.

SUSCEPTIBILITY TO ILLNESS. Fear of ill health breaks down the body's natural resistance and creates a favourable condition for any form of disease one may contact. The Fear of Ill Health often is related to the Fear of Poverty, especially in the case of the hypochondriac who constantly worries about the possibility of having to pay doctor's bills, hospital bills, etc. This type of person spends much time preparing for sickness, talking about death, saving money for cemetery lots, burial expenses, etc.

SELF-CODDLING. The habit of making a bid for sympathy using imaginary illness as the lure. (People often resort to this trick to avoid work.) The habit of feigning illness to cover plain laziness or to serve as an alibi for lack of ambition.

INTEMPERANCE. The habit of using alcohol or narcotics to deaden pains such as headaches, neuralgia, etc., instead of eliminating the cause. The habit of reading about illness and worrying over the possibility of being stricken by it. The habit of reading, listening to or viewing patent medicine advertisements.

THE FEAR OF LOSS OF LOVE

The original source of this inherent fear needs but little description. It obviously (on the male side) grew out of males' early and, apparently, inherently polygamous nature and the propensity to steal the mates of other males. It also derives (on the female side) from woman's maternal instincts and need for protection during periods of pregnancy and early child nurturing. Both men and women, therefore, have a biological and behavioural basis to fear the loss of love or 'mate companionship'.

Jealousy and other similar forms of neurosis thus grow out of human beings' inherited fear of the loss of security that the loss of love and companionship of another person represents. This fear is the most painful of all the Six Basic Fears. It plays more havoc with the body and mind than any of the other basic fears, and it can lead to severe mental problems.

As indicated above, the Fear of Loss of Love probably dates back to the Stone Age, when males stole females by brute force. They continue to do so in modern civilizations, but their technique has changed. Instead of force, they now use the lure of romantic persuasion, the promise of fine clothes, expensive automobiles and jewelry, access to economic power and other bait much more effective than physical force. Males' habits are the same as they were at the dawn of civilization, but are expressed differently.

Careful analysis has shown that women generally are more susceptible to the Fear of Loss of Love than are men. This fact is easily explained. Women through the ages have learned from experience that men, considered as a group, are polygamous by nature, that they are not to be trusted in the hands of rivals.

SYMPTOMS OF THE FEAR OF LOSS OF LOVE

The distinguishing symptoms of this fear are:

JEALOUSY. The habit of being suspicious of friends and loved ones without any reasonable evidence of sufficient grounds. (Jealousy is a form of neurosis which sometimes becomes violent without the slightest cause.) The habit of accusing wife or husband of infidelity without grounds. General suspicion of everyone, absolute faith in no one.

FAULT FINDING. The habit of finding fault with friends, relatives, business associates and loved ones upon the slightest provocation or without any cause whatsoever.

GAMBLING. The habit of gambling, stealing, cheating and otherwise taking risky chances to provide money for loved ones with the belief that love can be bought. The habit of spending beyond one's means or incurring debts to provide gifts for loved ones, with the object of making a favourable showing. Insomnia, nervousness, lack of persistence, weakness of will, lack of self-control, lack of self-reliance, bad temper.

THE FEAR OF OLD AGE

In the main, this fear grows out of two sources: First, the thought that old age may bring with it POVERTY. Secondly, and by far the most common source of origin, thoughts arising from false and cruel teachings of the past, which have been too well mixed with fire and brimstone and other 'bogeymen' cunningly designed to enslave people through fear.

In the basic Fear of Old Age, people have two very sound reasons for their apprehension—one growing out of their distrust of others, who may seize whatever worldly goods they may possess, and the other arising from the terrible pictures of the 'world beyond' which were planted in their minds through 'social heredity' before they came into full possession of their powers of reason.

The possibility of ill health, which is more common as people grow older, is also a contributing cause of this common Fear of Old Age. Eroticism also enters into the cause of the Fear of Old Age, as no one cherishes the thought of diminishing sexual attraction and activity.

The most common cause of Fear of Old Age is associated with the possibility of poverty. 'Poorhouse'—and everything the term conveys—is not a pretty word. It throws a chill into the mind of every person who faces the possibility of having to spend his or her declining years impoverished and worried constantly about meeting both the necessities of daily life and the special needs of old age.

Another contributing cause of the Fear of Old Age is the possibility of loss of freedom and independence, as old age may bring with it the loss of both physical and economic freedom.

SYMPTOMS OF THE FEAR OF OLD AGE

The commonest symptoms of this fear are:

THE TENDENCY TO SLOW DOWN and develop an inferiority complex at the age of mental maturity, around the age of 50, falsely believing oneself to be 'slipping' because of age. (The truth is that one's most useful years, mentally and spiritually, are those between 50 and 60.)

THE HABIT OF SPEAKING APOLOGETICALLY of oneself as being old merely because one has reached the age of 60 or 70, instead of reversing the rule and expressing gratitude for having reached the age of wisdom and understanding.

THE HABIT OF KILLING OFF INITIATIVE, imagination and self-reliance by falsely believing oneself too old to exercise these qualities. The habit of the man or woman of 50 or 60 dressing with the aim of trying to appear much younger and affecting mannerisms of youth, thereby inspiring ridicule by both friends and strangers.

THE FEAR OF DEATH

To some this is the cruellest of all the basic fears. The reason is obvious. In the majority of cases, the terrible pangs of fear associated with the thought of death may be charged directly to religious fanaticism. So called 'heathen' are less afraid of death than are the more civilized. For thousands of years, human beings have been asking the still unanswered questions, 'Whence?' and 'Whither?' 'Where did I come from, and where am I going?'

During the darker ages of history, the more cunning and

crafty were not slow to offer the answer to these questions—FOR A PRICE. Witness, now, the major source of the origin of the FEAR OF DEATH:

'Come into my tent, embrace my faith, accept my dogmas and I will give you a ticket that will admit you straightaway into heaven when you die,' cries a leader of sectarianism. 'Remain out of my tent,' says the same leader, 'and may the devil take you and burn you throughout eternity.'

ETERNITY is a long time. FIRE is a terrible thing. The thought of eternal punishment by fire not only causes people to fear death, it often causes them to lose their reason. It can destroy interest in life and make happiness impossible.

During my research I reviewed a book entitled *A Catalogue of the Gods* in which were listed the 30,000 gods which humankind has worshipped through the ages. Think of it! Thirty-thousand of them, represented by everything from a crawfish to a man. It is little wonder that people have become frightened at the approach of death.

While the religious leader may not be able to provide safe conduct into heaven, nor by lack of such provision force the unfortunate to descend into hell, the possibility of the latter seems so terrible that the very thought of it lays hold of the imagination in such a realistic way that it paralyses reason and sets up the Fear of Death.

In truth, NO ONE KNOWS for certain what heaven or hell is like or in what sense either exists. This very lack of positive knowledge opens the door of people's minds to the charlatans so that they may enter and control those minds with their stock of legerdemain and various brands of pious fraud and trickery.

The fear of DEATH is not as common now as it was during the age when there were no great colleges and universities. Scientists have turned the spotlight of truth upon the world, and this truth is rapidly freeing men and women from this terrible fear of DEATH. The young men and women who attend our colleges and universities are not so easily impressed by 'fire' and 'brimstone' any longer. Through the aid of biology, astronomy, geology and other related sciences, the fears of the dark ages that gripped the minds of humanity and destroyed people's reason have been dispelled.

Insane asylums have been filled with people who have gone mad because of the FEAR OF DEATH.

This fear is useless. Death will come no matter what anyone may think about it. Accept it as a necessity and pass the thought out of your mind. It must be a necessity or it would not come to all. Perhaps it is not as bad as it has been pictured.

The entire world is made up of only two things, ENERGY and MATTER. In elementary physics we learn that neither matter nor energy (the only two realities known) can be created or destroyed. Both matter and energy can be transformed, but neither can be destroyed.

Life is energy, if it is anything. If neither energy nor matter can be destroyed, then life cannot truly be destroyed. Life, like other forms of energy, may be passed through various processes of transition, or change, but it cannot be destroyed. Death is a mere transition.

But if death is *not* a mere change, or transition, then nothing comes after death except a long, eternal, peaceful sleep and sleep is nothing to be feared. Either way, you may thus wipe out forever the fear of death.

SYMPTOMS OF THE FEAR OF DEATH

The general symptom of this fear is the habit of THINKING about dying instead of making the most of LIFE, a habit which is due generally to lack of purpose or lack of a suitable occupation. This fear is more prevalent among the aged, but sometimes the more youthful are victims of it.

The greatest of all remedies for the Fear of Death is a BURNING DESIRE FOR ACHIEVEMENT, backed by useful service to others. Busy people seldom have time to think about dying. They find life too thrilling to worry about death. Sometimes the Fear of Death is closely associated with the Fear of Poverty, where one's death would leave loved ones poverty-stricken. In other cases, the Fear of Death is caused by illness and the consequent breaking down of physical body resistance. The commonest causes of the Fear of Death are poor health, poverty, lack of appropriate occupation, disappointment over love, insanity and religious fanaticism.

OLD MAN WORRY

Worry is a state of mind based upon fear. It works slowly but persistently. It is insidious and subtle. Step by step it digs itself in until it paralyses one's reasoning faculty and destroys self-confidence and initiative. Worry is a form of sustained fear caused by indecision, therefore, it is a state of mind which can be controlled.

An unsettled mind is helpless. Indecision makes an unsettled mind. Most individuals lack the willpower to reach decisions promptly and to stand by them after they have been made, even during normal business conditions. During periods of economic distress (such as the world has recently experienced), individuals are handicapped not solely by their inherent nature to be slow at reaching decisions, but by the influence of the *indecision of others around them* who have created a state of mass indecision.

During an international economic downturn, the whole

atmosphere all over the world can be filled with 'Fearenza' and 'Worryitis', two mental disease germs which can spread rapidly. There is only one known antidote for these germs. It is the habit of prompt and firm DECISION. Moreover, it is an antidote which every individual must apply for himself or herself.

We do not worry over conditions once we have reached a decision to follow a *definite line of action*. I once interviewed a man who was to be electrocuted two hours later. The condemned man was the calmest of some eight men who were on death row with him. His calmness prompted me to ask him how it felt to know that he was going into eternity in a short while. With a smile of confidence on his face, he said, 'It feels fine. Just think, brother, my troubles will soon be over. I have had nothing but trouble all my life. It has been a hardship to get food and clothing. Soon I will not need these things. I have felt fine ever since I learned FOR CERTAIN that I must die. I made up my mind then to accept my fate in good spirit.'

As he spoke he devoured a dinner of proportions sufficient for three men, eating every mouthful of the food brought to him and apparently enjoying it as much as if no disaster awaited him. DECISION gave this man resignation to his fate! Decision can also prevent one's acceptance of undesired circumstances.

Through indecision, the Six Basic Fears become translated into a state of worry and anxiety. Relieve yourself *forever* of the Fear of Death by reaching a decision to accept death as an inescapable event. Whip the Fear of Poverty by reaching a decision to get along with whatever wealth you can accumulate WITHOUT WORRY. Put your foot upon the neck of the Fear of Criticism by reaching a decision NOT TO WORRY about what other people think, do or say. Eliminate the Fear of Old Age by reaching a decision to accept it not as a handicap, but as a great blessing which carries with it wisdom, self-control and understanding not known to youth. Acquit yourself of the Fear of Ill Health by the decision to forget symptoms. Master the Fear of Loss of Love by reaching a decision to get along without love if that is necessary.

Kill the habit of worry in all its forms by reaching a general, blanket decision that nothing which life has to offer is worth the price of worry. With this decision will come poise, peace of mind, and calmness of thought which will bring happiness.

Those whose minds are filled with fear not only destroy their own chances of intelligent action, but they transmit these destructive vibrations to the minds of all who come into contact with them and destroy also their chances.

Even a dog or a horse knows when its master lacks courage. Moreover, a dog or a horse will pick up the vibrations of fear thrown off by its master and behave accordingly. Lower down the line of intelligence in the animal kingdom, one finds this same capacity to pick up the vibrations of fear. The vibrations of fear pass from one mind to another just as quickly and as surely as the sound of the human voice passes from the broadcasting station to the receiving set of a radio.

The person who gives expression, by word of mouth, to negative or destructive thoughts is practically certain to experience the results of those words in the form of a destructive kickback. The release of destructive thought impulses alone, without the aid of words, produces also a kickback in more ways than one. First of all, and perhaps most important to be remembered, the person who releases thoughts of a destructive nature must suffer damage through the breaking down of the faculty of Creative Imagination. Secondly, the presence in the mind of any destructive emotion develops a negative personality which repels people and often converts them into antagonists. The third source of damage to the person who entertains or releases negative thoughts lies in this significant fact: negative thought impulses are not only damaging to others, but they also EMBED THEMSELVES IN THE SUBCONSCIOUS MIND OF THE PERSON

RELEASING THEM and there become a part of his or her character.

One is never through with a thought, merely by releasing it. When a thought is released, it spreads in every direction, but it also plants itself permanently in the subconscious mind of the person releasing it.

Your business in life is presumably to achieve success. To be successful, you must find peace of mind, acquire the material needs of life, and above all, attain HAPPINESS. All of these evidences of success begin in the form of thought impulses.

You may control your own mind. You have the power to feed it whatever thought impulses you choose. With this privilege goes also the responsibility of using it constructively. You are the master of your own earthly destiny just as surely as you have the power to control your own thoughts. You may influence, direct, and eventually control your own environment, making your life what you want it to be—or you may neglect to exercise the privilege which is yours to make your life to order, thus casting yourself upon the broad 'Sea of Circumstance', where you will be tossed hither and yon like a chip on the waves of the ocean.

THE DEVIL'S WORKSHOP

The Seventh Basic Evil

In addition to the Six Basic Fears, there is another evil by which people suffer. It constitutes a rich soil in which the seeds of failure grow abundantly. It is so subtle that its presence often is not detected. This affliction cannot properly be classed as a fear. IT IS MORE DEEPLY SEATED AND MORE OFTEN FATAL THAN ALL OF THE SIX FEARS. For want of a better name, let us call this evil the SUSCEPTIBILITY TO NEGATIVE INFLUENCES.

Individuals who accumulate great riches always protect themselves against this evil! The poverty stricken never do! Those who succeed in any calling must prepare their minds to resist the evil. If you are reading this philosophy for the purpose of accumulating riches in whatever form, you should examine yourself very carefully to determine whether you are susceptible to negative influences. If you neglect this self-analysis, you will forfeit your right to attain the object of your desires.

Make the analysis searching. After you read the questions prepared for this self-analysis, hold yourself to a strict accounting in your answers. Go at the task as carefully as you would search for any other enemy you knew to be awaiting you in ambush and deal with your own faults as you would with a more tangible enemy.

You can easily protect yourself against robbers because the law provides organized cooperation for your benefit, but the 'Seventh Basic Evil' is more difficult to master because it strikes when you are not aware of its presence, when you are asleep and while you are awake. Moreover, its weapon is intangible because it consists of merely a STATE OF MIND. This evil is also dangerous because it strikes in as many different forms as there are human experiences. Sometimes it enters the mind through the well-meant words of one's own relatives. At other times it bores from within, through one's own mental attitude. Always it is as deadly as poison, even though it may not kill as quickly.

HOW TO PROTECT YOURSELF AGAINST NEGATIVE INFLUENCES

To protect yourself against negative influences, whether of your own making or the result of the activities and thoughts of negative people around you, recognize that you have WILLPOWER and put it into constant use until it builds a wall of immunity against negative influences in your own mind.

Recognize the fact that you and every other human being are by nature lazy, indifferent and susceptible to all suggestions that harmonize with your weaknesses.

Recognize that you are, by nature, susceptible to all the Six Basic Fears, and set up habits for the purpose of counteracting all these fears.

Recognize that negative influences often work on you through your subconscious mind, therefore, they are difficult to detect, and keep your mind closed against all people who depress or discourage you in any way.

Clean out your medicine chest, throw away all pill bottles, and stop pandering to colds, aches, pains and imaginary illness.

Deliberately seek the company of people who influence you to THINK AND ACT FOR YOURSELF.

Do not EXPECT troubles, as they have a tendency not to disappoint.

Without doubt, the most common weakness of all human beings is the habit of leaving their minds open to the negative influence of other people. This weakness is all the more damaging because most people do not recognize that they are cursed by it, and many who acknowledge it neglect or refuse to correct the evil until it becomes an uncontrollable part of their daily habits.

> **POINTS TO REMEMBER**
>
> 1. Beware of the three negatives that will hinder your path.
> 2. Fears are nothing more than states of mind.
> 3. Thought impulses begin immediately to translate themselves into their physical equivalent.

9

THE MASTERY OF POVERTY

POVERTY is the result of a negative condition of the mind, which practically every living person experiences at one time or another. It is the first and the most disastrous of the seven basic fears, but it is only a state of mind, and like the other six fears, it is subject to the control of the individual.

The fact that a major portion of all people are born in surroundings of poverty, *accept it as inescapable*, and go with it all through their lives, indicates how potent a factor it is in the lives of people. It may well be that poverty is one of the testing devices with which the Creator separates the weak from the strong, for it is a notable fact that those who master poverty, become rich not only in material things, *but also rich and often wise in spiritual values as well.*

I have observed that men who have mastered poverty invariably have a keen sense of Faith in their ability to master practically everything else which stands in the way of their progress; while those who have accepted poverty as inescapable show signs of weakness in many other directions. In no case have I known anyone who had accepted poverty as unavoidable, who had not failed also to exercise that great Gift of the power to take possession of his own mind-power (as the Creator intended all people should do).

All people go through testing periods throughout their lives, under many circumstances, which clearly disclose whether or not they have accepted and used that Great Gift of exclusive control over their own mind-power. And I have observed that along with this Great Gift from the Infinite go also definite penalties for neglect to embrace and use the Gift, and definite rewards for its recognition and use.

One of the more important rewards for its use consists in complete freedom from the entire seven basic fears and all the lesser fears, with full access to the magic power of FAITH to take the place of these fears.

The penalties for neglect to embrace and use this Great Gift are legion. In addition to all of the seven basic fears, there are many other liabilities not included with these fears. One of the major penalties for failure to use the Great Gift is *the total impossibility of attaining peace of mind.*

Poverty has many merits if and when an individual relates himself to it in a positive mental attitude instead of submitting to it in the false belief that it is unavoidable, or the lazy attitude that it is not worth fighting off. Poverty may be one of the devices with which the Creator forces man to sharpen his wits, arouse his enthusiasm, act on his personal initiative and make a determined fight against the forces which oppose him, in order that he may survive.

Poverty may also be a device of the Creator by which he manoeuvres man into a state of mind where he finally *discovers himself from within.* In a great country like the United States of America there is no valid reason for any able-minded person to accept and become bound to slavery through poverty. Here, as nowhere else in the world, is a training ground for personal freedom, which offers every individual the best of all possible opportunities to embrace and use this Great Gift of the *right to pattern his own earthly destiny and attain it.* And here, as nowhere else, has the individual been provided with every conceivable motive for embracing and using the Great Gift. The payoff is so great that the individual may literally 'write his own ticket'.

The best evidence that Destiny smiles on those who are born to poverty consists in the well-recognized fact that too seldom does an individual who is born to great wealth ever make any worthy contributions to the world which make it a better place for mankind. Many children of very rich people, who never have the benefit of the seasoning influence of poverty or struggle, often grow up 'soft' and lacking in the necessary endurance or the motive to make themselves useful.

When fortune does smile upon a person who has great wealth, she generally chooses only those who created their wealth through useful service—not those who inherited it or procured it through means which brought injury to others. Fortune definitely frowns upon all ill-gotten wealth, *and often causes it to mysteriously evaporate.*

POVERTY IS A STATE OF MIND

Whether poverty becomes a curse or a blessing depends entirely upon the way the individual relates himself to it. If it is accepted in a spirit of meekness, as an unavoidable handicap, then it becomes just that. If poverty is accepted as a mere challenge to the individual to fight his way through and master, then it becomes a blessing—in fact, one of the great miracles of life. Poverty may become either a stumbling-block or a stepping-stone on which he may rise to whatever heights of achievement he may set his heart upon, depending entirely on his attitude toward it and his *reactions to it.*

Both poverty and riches consist in a state of mind! They follow precisely the pattern the individual creates and visualizes by the dominating thoughts he expresses. Thoughts of poverty attract their material counterpart. Thoughts of riches likewise attract their material counterpart. The law of *harmonious attraction* translates all thoughts into their kindred material counterparts. This great truth explains why the majority of people experience unhappiness and poverty throughout their lives. They allow their minds to fear unhappiness and poverty, and their dominating thoughts are on these circumstances. The law of harmonious attraction takes over and brings them *that which they expect.*

When I was a small boy, I heard a very dramatic speech on the subject of poverty which made a lasting impression upon my mind, and I am sure that speech was responsible for my determination to master poverty despite the fact that I had been born in poverty and had never known anything except poverty. The speech came from my stepmother shortly after she came to our home and took over one of the most forlorn, poverty-stricken places I have ever known.

The speech was as follows:

> This place which we call home is a disgrace to all of us and a handicap for our children. We are all able-bodied people and there is no need for us to accept poverty when we know that it is the result of nothing but laziness or indifference.
>
> If we stay here and accept the conditions under which we now live, our children will grow up and accept these conditions also. I do not like poverty; I have never accepted poverty as my lot, and I shall not accept it now!
>
> For the moment I do not know what our first step

will be in our break for freedom from poverty, but this much I do know—we shall make that break successfully, no matter how long it may take or how many sacrifices we may have to make. I intend that our children shall have the advantage of good educations, *but more than this, I intend that they shall be inspired with the ambition to master poverty.*

Poverty is a disease which, once it is accepted, becomes a fixation which is hard to shake off.

It is no disgrace to be born in poverty but it most decidedly is a disgrace to accept this birth right as irrevocable.

We live in the richest and the greatest country civilization has yet produced. Here opportunity beckons to everyone who has the ambition to recognize and embrace it, and as far as this family is concerned, if opportunity does not beckon to us, *we shall create our own opportunity to escape this sort of life.*

Poverty is like creeping paralysis! Slowly it destroys the desire for freedom, strips one of the ambition to enjoy better things of life and undermines personal initiative. Also, it conditions one's mind for the acceptance of myriad fears, including the fear of ill health, the fear of criticism and the fear of physical pain.

Our children are too young to know the dangers of accepting poverty as their lot, but I shall see to it that they are made conscious of these dangers, and I shall see to it also that they become prosperity conscious, *that they expect prosperity and become willing to pay the price of prosperity.*

I have quoted this speech from memory, but it is substantially what my stepmother said to my father in my presence shortly after they were married. That 'first step' in the break from poverty, which she mentioned in her speech, came when my stepmother inspired my father to enter Louisville Dental College and became a dentist, and paid for his training with the life insurance money she received from the death of her first husband.

With the income from that investment in my father, she sent her three children and my younger brother through college and started each of them on the road to mastery of poverty.

As for myself, she was instrumental in placing me in a position where the late Andrew Carnegie gave me an opportunity such as no other author ever received—an opportunity which permitted me to learn from more than five hundred of the top-ranking, successful men who collaborated with me in giving the world a practical philosophy of personal achievement. A philosophy based on the 'know-how' of my collaborators, gained from their lifetime experiences.

While it is estimated that my personal contribution to posterity has benefitted many millions of people, throughout two-thirds of the world, the credit for this accomplishment really dates back to that historic speech of my stepmother's, in which she disavowed poverty.

We see, therefore, that poverty can be the means of inspiring one to plan and achieve profound objectives. My stepmother did not fear poverty, but she disliked it and refused to accept it. And somehow the Creator seems to favour those who *know precisely what they want and what they do not want.* My stepmother was one of that type. If she had accepted poverty, or had she feared poverty, the lines you are now reading never would have been written.

Poverty is a great experience, but it is something to experience and then master before it breaks the will to be free and independent. The person who has never experienced poverty is to be pitied, perhaps, but the person who has experienced poverty and has accepted it as his lot is more to be pitied, for he has thereby condemned himself to eternal bondage.

Most of the truly great men and women throughout civilization have known poverty, but they experienced it, renounced it, mastered it and made themselves free. Otherwise, they never would have become great. Anyone who accepts from life anything he does not want is not free. The Creator has provided everyone with the means of determining very largely his own earthly destiny, which consists in the privilege of freeing himself from those things which are not desirable.

Poverty can be a profound blessing. It can also be a lifelong curse. The determining factor as to which it shall be consists in one's mental attitude toward it. If it is accepted as a challenge to greater effort, it is a blessing. If it is accepted as an unavoidable handicap, then it is an enduring curse.

POINTS TO REMEMBER

1. Poverty is a negative state of mind.
2. The seven basic fears and how to overpower them.
3. Use poverty to discover yourself from within.

10

THE HABIT OF SAVING

To advise one to save money without describing how to save would be somewhat like drawing the picture of a horse and writing under it, 'This is a horse.' It is obvious to all that the saving of money is one of the essentials for success, but the big question uppermost in the minds of the majority of those who do not save is:

'How can I do it?'

The saving of money is solely a matter of habit. For this reason, this lesson begins with a brief analysis of the Law of Habit.

It is literally true that man, through the Law of Habit, shapes his own personality. Through repetition, any act indulged in a few times becomes a habit, and the mind appears to be nothing more than a mass of motivating forces growing out of our daily habits.

When once fixed in the mind a habit voluntarily impels one to action. For example, follow a given route to your daily work, or to some other place that you frequently visit, and very soon the habit has been formed and your mind will lead you over that route without thought on your part. Moreover, if you start out with the intention of traveling in another direction, without keeping the thought of the change in routes constantly in mind, you will find yourself following the old route.

Public speakers have found that the telling over and over again of a story, which may be based upon pure fiction, brings into play the Law of Habit, and very soon they forget whether the story is true or not.

WALLS OF LIMITATION BUILT THROUGH HABIT

Millions of people go through life in poverty and want because they have made destructive use of the Law of Habit. Not understanding either the Law of Habit or the Law of Attraction through which 'like attracts like', those who remain in poverty seldom realize that they are where they are as the result of their own acts.

Fix in your mind the thought that your ability is limited to a given earning capacity and you will never earn more than that, because the law of habit will set up a definite limitation of the amount you can earn, your subconscious mind will accept this limitation, and very soon you will feel yourself 'slipping' until finally you will become so hedged in by FEAR OF POVERTY (one of the six basic fears) that opportunity will no longer knock at your door; your doom will be sealed; your fate fixed.

Formation of the Habit of Saving does not mean that you shall limit your earning capacity; it means just the opposite—that you shall apply this law so that it not only conserves that which you earn, in a systematic manner, but it also places you in the way of greater opportunity and gives you the vision, the self-confidence, the imagination, the enthusiasm, the initiative and leadership actually to increase your earning capacity.

'WE TALK AND THINK ONLY OF ABUNDANCE HERE. IF YOU HAVE A TALE OF WOE PLEASE KEEP IT, AS WE DO NOT WANT IT.'

No business firm wants the services of a pessimist, and those who understand the Law of Attraction and the Law of Habit will no more tolerate the pessimist than they would permit a burglar to roam around their place of business, for the reason that one such person will destroy the usefulness of those around him.

In tens of thousands of homes, the general topic of conversation is poverty and want, and that is just what they are getting. They think of poverty, they talk of poverty, they accept poverty as their lot in life. They reason that because their ancestors were poor before them they, also, must remain poor.

The poverty consciousness is formed as the result of the habit of thinking of and fearing poverty. 'Lo! the thing I had feared has come upon me.'

THE SLAVERY OF DEBT

Debt is a merciless master, a fatal enemy of the savings habit.

Poverty, alone, is sufficient to kill off ambition, destroy self-confidence and destroy hope, but add to it the burden of debt and all who are victims of these two cruel task-masters are practically doomed to failure.

No man can do his best work, no man can express himself in terms that command respect, no man can either create or carry out a definite purpose in life, with heavy debt hanging over his head. The man who is bound in the slavery of debt is just as helpless as the slave who is bound by ignorance, or by actual chains.

A very close friend has an income of $1,000 a month. His wife loves 'society' and tries to make a $20,000 showing on a $12,000 income, with the result that this poor fellow is usually about $8,000 in debt. Every member of his family has the 'spending habit', having acquired this from the mother. The children, two girls and one boy, are now of the age when they are thinking of going to college, but this is impossible because of the father's debts. The result is dissension between the father and his children which makes the entire family unhappy and miserable.

It is a terrible thing even to think of going through life like a prisoner in chains, bound down and owned by somebody else on account of debt. The accumulation of debt is a habit. It starts in a small way and grows to enormous proportions slowly, step by step, until finally it takes charge of one's very soul.

Thousands of young men start their married lives with unnecessary debts hanging over their heads and never manage to get out from under the load. After the novelty of marriage begins to wear off (as it usually does) the married couple begin to feel the embarrassment of want, and this feeling grows until it leads, oftentimes, to open dissatisfaction with one another, and eventually to the divorce court.

A man who is bound by the slavery of debt has no time or inclination to set up or work out ideals, with the result that he drifts downward with time until he eventually begins to set up limitations in his own mind, and by these he hedges himself behind prison walls of FEAR and doubt from which he never escapes. No sacrifice is too great to avoid the misery of debt!

'Think of what you owe yourself and those who are dependent upon you and resolve to be no man's debtor,' is the advice of one very successful man whose early chances were destroyed by debt. This man came to himself soon enough to throw off the habit of buying that which he did not need and eventually worked his way out of slavery.

Most men who develop the habit of debt will not be so fortunate as to come to their senses in time to save themselves, because debt is something like quicksand in that it has a tendency to draw its victim deeper and deeper into the mire.

The Fear of Poverty is one of the most destructive of the six basic fears described in Lesson Three. The man who becomes hopelessly in debt is seized with this poverty fear, his ambition and self-confidence become paralysed, and he sinks gradually into oblivion.

There are two classes of debts, and these are so different in nature that they deserve to be here described, as follows:

1. There are debts incurred for luxuries which become a dead loss.
2. There are debts incurred in the course of professional or business trading which represent service or merchandise that can be converted back into assets.

The first class of debts is the one to be avoided. The second class may be indulged in, providing the one incurring the debts uses judgment and does not go beyond the bounds of reasonable limitation. The moment one buys beyond his limitations he enters the realm of speculation, and speculation swallows more of its victims than it enriches.

Practically all people who live beyond their means are tempted to speculate with the hope that they may recoup, at a single turn of the wheel of fortune, so to speak, their entire indebtedness. The wheel generally stops at the wrong place and, far from finding themselves out of debt, such people as indulge in speculation are bound more closely as slaves of debt.

The Fear of Poverty breaks down the willpower of its

victims, and they then find themselves unable to restore their lost fortunes, and, what is still more sad, they lose all ambition to extricate themselves from the slavery of debt.

Hardly a day passes that one may not see an account in the newspapers of at least one suicide as the result of worry over debts. The slavery of debt causes more suicides every year than all other causes combined, which is a slight indication of the cruelty of the poverty fear.

During the war millions of men faced the front-line trenches without flinching, knowing that death might overtake them any moment. Those same men, when facing the Fear of Poverty, often cringe and out of sheer desperation, which paralyses their reason, sometimes commit suicide.

The person who is free from debt may whip poverty and achieve outstanding financial success, but, if he is bound by debt, such achievement is but a remote possibility, and never a probability.

Fear of Poverty is a negative, destructive state of mind. Moreover, one negative state of mind has a tendency to attract other similar states of mind. For example, the Fear of Poverty may attract the fear of III Health, and these two may attract the hear of Old Age, so that the victim finds himself poverty-stricken, in ill health and actually growing old long before the time when he should begin to show the signs of old age. Millions of untimely, nameless graves have been filled by this cruel state of mind known as the Fear of Poverty!

Less than a dozen years ago a young man held a responsible position with the City National Bank, of New York City. Through living beyond his income he contracted a large amount of debts which caused him to worry until this destructive habit began to show up in his work and he was dismissed from the bank's service.

He secured another position, at less money, but his creditors embarrassed him so that he decided to resign and go away into another city, where he hoped to escape them until he had accumulated enough money to pay off his indebtedness. Creditors have a way of tracing debtors, so very soon they were close on the heels of this young man, whose employer found out about his indebtedness and dismissed him from his position.

He then searched in vain for employment for two months. One cold night he went to the top of one of the tall buildings on Broadway and jumped off. Debt had claimed another victim.

HOW TO MASTER THE FEAR OF POVERTY

To whip the Fear of Poverty one must take two very definite steps, providing one is in debt. First, quit the habit of buying on credit and follow this by gradually paying off the debts that you have already incurred.

Being free from the worry of indebtedness you are ready to revamp the habits of your mind and redirect your course toward prosperity. Adopt, as a part of your definite chief aim, the habit of saving a regular proportion of your income, even if this be no more than a penny a day. Very soon this habit will begin to lay hold of your mind and you will actually get joy out of saving.

Any habit may be discontinued by building in its place some other and more desirable habit. The 'spending' habit must be replaced by the 'saving' habit by all who attain financial independence.

Merely to discontinue an undesirable habit is not enough, as such habits have a tendency to reappear unless the place they formerly occupied in the mind is filled by some other habit of a different nature.

The discontinuance of a habit leaves a 'hole' in the mind, and this hole must be filled up with some other form of habit or the old one will return and claim its place.

Throughout this course many psychological formulas, which the student has been requested to memorize and practice, have been described.

These formulas may be assimilated so they become a part of your mental machinery, through the Law of Habit, if you will follow the instructions for their use which accompany each of them.

It is assumed that you are striving to attain financial independence. The accumulation of money is not difficult after you have mastered the Fear of Poverty and developed in its place the Habit of Saving.

The author of this course would be greatly disappointed to know that any student of the course got the impression from anything in this or any of the other: lessons that Success is measured by dollars alone.

However, money does represent an important factor in success, and it must be given its proper value in any philosophy intended to help people in becoming useful, happy and prosperous.

The cold, cruel, relentless truth is that in this age of materialism a man is no more than so many grains of sand, which may be blown helter-skelter by every stray wind of circumstance, unless he is entrenched behind the power of money!

Genius may offer many rewards to those who possess it, but the fact still remains that genius without money with which to give it expression is but an empty, skeleton-like honour.

The man without money is at the mercy of the man who has it!

And this goes, regardless of the amount of ability he may possess, the training he has had or the native genius with which he was gifted by nature.

There is no escape from the fact that people will weigh you very largely in the light of bank balances, no matter who you are or what you can do. The first question that arises, in the minds of most people, when they meet a stranger, is, 'How much money has he?' If he has money he is welcomed into homes and business opportunities are thrown his way. All sorts of attention are lavished upon him. He is a prince, and as such is entitled to the best of the land.

But if his shoes are run down at the heels, his clothes are not pressed, his collar is dirty and he shows plainly the signs of impoverished finances, woe be his lot, for the passing crowd will step on his toes and blow the smoke of disrespect in his face.

These are not pretty statements, but they have one virtue—THEY ARE TRUE!

This tendency to judge people by the money they have, or their power to control money, is not confined to any one class of people. We all have a touch of it, whether we recognize the fact or not.

Thomas A. Edison is one of the best known and most respected inventors in the world, yet it is no misstatement of facts to say that he would have remained a practically unknown, obscure personage had he not followed the habit of conserving his resources and shown his ability to save money.

Henry Ford never would have got to first base with his 'horseless carriage' had he not developed, quite early in life, the habit of saving. Moreover, had Mr Ford not conserved his resources and hedged himself behind their power he would have been 'swallowed up' by his competitors or those who covetously desired to take his business away from him, long,

long years ago.

Many a man has gone a very long way toward success, only to stumble and fall, never again to rise, because of lack of money in times of emergency. The mortality rate in business each year, due to lack of reserve capital for emergencies, is stupendous. To this one cause are due more of the business failures than to all other causes combined!

Reserve Funds are essential in the successful operation of business!

Likewise, Savings Accounts are essential to success on the part of individuals. Without a savings fund the individual suffers in two ways: first, by inability to seize opportunities that come only to the person with some ready cash, and, second, by embarrassment due to some unexpected emergency calling for cash.

It might be said, also, that the individual suffers in still a third respect by not developing the Habit of Saving, through lack of certain other qualities essential for success which grow out of the practice of the Habit of Saving.

The nickels, dimes and pennies which the average person allows to slip through his fingers would, if systematically saved and properly put to work, eventually bring financial independence.

Through the courtesy of a prominent Building and Loan Association the following table has been compiled, showing what a monthly saving of $5.00, $10.00, $25.00 or $50.00 will amount to at the end of ten years. These figures are startling when one comes to consider the fact that the average person spends from $5.00 to $50.00 a month for useless merchandise or so-called 'entertainment'.

HOW MUCH SHOULD ONE SAVE?

The first question that will arise is, 'How much should one save?' The answer cannot be given in a few words, for the amount one should save depends upon many conditions, some of which may be within one's control and some of which may not be.

Generally speaking, a man who works for a salary should apportion his income about as follows:

Savings Account	20%
Living—Clothes, Food and Shelter	50%
Education	10%
Recreation	10%
Life Insurance	10%
	100%

The following, however, indicates the approximate distribution which the average man actually makes of his income:

Savings Account	Nothing
Living—Clothes, Food and Shelter	60%
Education	0%
Recreation	35%
Life Insurance	5%
	100%

Under the item of 'recreation' is included, of course, many expenditures that do not really 'recreate', such as money spent for alcoholic drinks, dinner parties and other similar items which may actually serve to undermine one's health and destroy character.

An experienced analyst of men has stated that he could tell very accurately, by examining a man's monthly budget, what sort of a life the man is living; moreover, that he will get most of his information from the one item of 'recreation.' This, then, is an item to be watched as carefully as the greenhouse keeper watches the thermometer which controls the life and death of his plants.

Those who keep budget accounts often include an item called 'entertainment', which, in a majority of cases, turns out to be an evil because it depletes the income heavily and when carried to excess depletes, also, the health. We are living, right now, in an age when the item of 'entertainment' is altogether too high in most budget allowances. Tens of thousands of people who earn not more than $50.00 a week are spending as much as one third of their incomes for what they call 'entertainment', which comes in a bottle, with a questionable label on it, at anywhere from $6.00 to $12.00 a quart. Not only are these unwise people wasting the money that should go into a savings fund, but, of far greater danger, they are destroying both character and health.

Nothing in this lesson is intended as a preachment on morality or on any other subject. We are here dealing with cold facts which, to a large extent, constitute the building materials out of which SUCCESS may be created.

However, this is an appropriate place to state some FACTS which have such a direct bearing on the subject of achieving success that they cannot be omitted without weakening this entire course in general and this lesson in particular.

We are all victims of HABIT!

Unfortunately for most of us, we are reared by parents who have no conception whatsoever of the psychology of habit, and, without being aware of their fault, most parents aid and abet their offspring in the development of the spending habit by overindulgence with spending money, and by lack of training in the Habit of Saving.

The habits of early childhood cling to us all through life.

Fortunate, indeed, is the child whose parents have the foresight and the understanding of the value, as a character builder, of the Habit of Saving, to inculcate this habit in the minds of their children.

It is a training that yields rich rewards.

Give the average man $100.00 that he did not contemplate receiving, and what will he do with it? Why, he will begin to cogitate in his own mind on how he can SPEND the money. Dozens of things that he needs, or THINKS he needs, will flash into his mind, but it is a rather safe bet that it will never occur to him (unless he has acquired the savings habit) to make this $100.00 the beginning of a savings account. Before night comes, he will have the $100.00 spent, or at least he will have decided in his mind how he is going to SPEND IT, thus adding more fuel to the already too bright flame of Habit of Spending.

We are ruled by our habits!

It requires force of character, determination and power of firm DECISION to open a savings account and then add to it a regular, if small, portion of all subsequent income.

There is one rule by which any man may determine, well in advance, whether or not he will ever enjoy the financial freedom and independence which is so universally desired by all men, and this rule has absolutely nothing to do with the amount of one's income.

The rule is that if a man follows the systematic habit of saving a definite proportion of all money he earns or receives in other ways, he is practically sure to place himself in a position of financial independence. If he saves nothing, he IS ABSOLUTELY SURE NEVER TO BE FINANCIALLY INDEPENDENT, no matter how much his income may be.

The one and only exception to this rule is that a man who does not save might possibly inherit such a large sum of money that he could not spend it, or he might inherit it under a trust which would protect it for him, but these eventualities are rather remote; so much so, in fact, that YOU cannot rely upon such a miracle happening to you.

POINTS TO REMEMBER

1. Mindset to make saving money a habit.
2. The poverty consciousness is formed as the result of the habit of thinking of and fearing poverty.
3. Beware of the merciless trap of debt.

11

THE 17 PRINCIPLES OF SUCCESS

The list that follows is meant to serve as a reminder. Look it over once a week. Are you making regular progress in each of these areas? If you routinely evaluate your efforts to embrace the principles, you are less likely to be caught in a crisis because you've neglected to think accurately, for instance, or to find that your co-workers suddenly regard you as an opportunistic shark.

1. Develop definiteness of purpose
2. Establish a mastermind alliance
3. Assemble an attractive personality
4. Use applied faith
5. Go the extra mile
6. Create personal initiative
7. Build a positive mental attitude
8. Control your enthusiasm
9. Enforce self-discipline
10. Think accurately
11. Control your attention
12. Inspire teamwork
13. Learn from adversity and defeat
14. Cultivate creative vision
15. Maintain sound health

16. Budget your time and money
17. Use cosmic habitforce

A DETAILED EVALUATION

Following are concise summaries of the steps to making each principle a part of your life. Read them through and then use the lines provided at the end of each section to write down specific actions you plan to take to implement the principles.

The summaries themselves will give you concrete recommendations about what to do. Under the definiteness of purpose you might write down that you will define your major goal, write out a plan for achieving it, and read that plan aloud to yourself every day, all of which are mentioned in the summary. But if you also include a date by which you will have your plan written down, you will be making a commitment to yourself that will provide you with extra motivation. So do not simply parrot back the summary's suggestions; consider carefully the changes you need to make and be as detailed as possible in writing them out. In a few weeks or months you can look at these notes, recognize the progress you've made, and renew your commitment to success.

1. DEVELOP DEFINITENESS OF PURPOSE—WITH PMA

The Starting Point of All Worthwhile Achievements

You should have one high, desirable, outstanding goal and keep it ever before you. You can have many nonconflicting goals which help you to reach your major definite goal. It is advisable to have immediate, intermediate and distant objectives. When you set a definite major goal, you are apt to recognize that which will help you achieve it.

Determine or fix in your mind exactly what you desire. Be definite.

Evaluate and determine exactly what you will give in return.

Set a definite date for exactly when you intend to possess your desire.

Identify your desire with a definite plan for carrying out and achieving your objective. Put your plan into action at once.

Clearly define your plan for achievement. Write out precisely and concisely exactly what you want, exactly when you want to achieve it and exactly what you intend to give in return.

Each and every day, morning and evening, read your written statement aloud. As you read it, see, feel and believe yourself already in possession of your objective.

Engage in personal inspection with regularity to determine whether you are on the right track and headed in the right direction so that you don't deviate from the path that leads to the achievement of your objective.

To guarantee success, engage daily in study, thinking and planning time with PMA regarding yourself and your family and how you can achieve your definite goals.

WHATEVER YOUR MIND CAN CONCEIVE AND BELIEVE, YOU CAN ACHIEVE—WHEN YOU HAVE PMA AND APPLY IT.

My commitment to use this principle in my life is:

_____
_____
_____
_____

2. ESTABLISH A MASTERMIND ALLIANCE—WITH PMA

A mastermind alliance is two or more minds working together in the spirit of perfect harmony toward the attainment of a specific objective.

This principle makes it possible for you, through association with others, to acquire and utilize the knowledge and experience needed for the attainment of any desired goal in

Your mastermind alliance can be created by surrounding yourself or aligning yourself with the advice, counsel and personal cooperation of several people who are willing to lend you their wholehearted aid for the attainment of your objective in the spirit of perfect harmony.

You can create a mastermind alliance with your spouse, your manager, a friend, a co-worker, etc. Once a mastermind alliance is formed, the group as a whole must become and remain active. The group must move in a definite plan, at a definite time, toward a definite common objective. Indecision, inactivity or delay will destroy usefulness of the alliance. There must be a complete meeting of the minds without reservations on the part of any member.

You can have several mastermind alliances, each with different objectives—i.e., an alliance with your spouse to reach your family objectives, an alliance with your banker or investment counsellor or attorney for your financial objectives, an alliance with your minister or clergy for your spiritual objectives, etc.

My commitment to use this principle in my life is:

_____
_____
_____
_____

3. ASSEMBLE AN ATTRACTIVE PERSONALITY— WITH PMA

Your personality is your greatest asset or greatest liability, for it embraces everything that you control: mind, body and soul. A person's personality is the person. It shapes the nature of your thoughts, your deeds, your relationships with others and it establishes the boundaries of the space you occupy in the world.

It is essential that you develop a pleasing personality—pleasing to yourself and to others.

It is imperative that you develop the habit of being sensitive to your own reactions to individuals, circumstances and events and to the reactions of individuals and groups to what you say, think or do.

POSITIVE FACTORS OF A PLEASING PERSONALITY

- A positive mental attitude
- Tolerance
- Alertness
- Common courtesy
- A fondness for people
- Flexibility
- Tactfulness
- Personal magnetism
- Smiling
- Enthusiasm
- Control of temper and emotions
- Patience
- Proper dress
- A pleasant tone of voice
- Control of facial expressions
- Sportsmanship
- Sincerity
- A sense of humour
- Humility of the heart

DO UNTO OTHERS AS YOU WOULD HAVE OTHERS DO UNTO YOU.

My commitment to use this principle in my life is:

_____
_____
_____
_____

4. USE APPLIED FAITH—WITH PMA

Faith is a state of mind through which your aims, desires, plans and purposes may be translated into their physical or financial equivalent.

Applied faith means action—specifically, the habit of applying your faith under any and all circumstances. It is faith in your God, yourself, your fellowman—and the unlimited opportunities available to you.

Faith without action is dead. Faith is the art of believing by doing. It comes as a result of persistent action. Fear and doubt are faith in reverse gear. Faith, in its positive application, is the key which will give one direct communication with Infinite Intelligence.

Applied faith is belief in an objective or purpose backed by unqualified activity. If you want results, try a prayer. When you pray, express your gratitude, and thanksgiving for the blessings you already have received; then ask the Good Lord for his help. Affirm the objectives of your desires through prayer each night and morning. Inspire your imagination to see yourself already in possession of them, and act precisely as if you were already in physical possession of them. The possession of anything first takes place mentally by being imagined in the mind's eye.

PRAYER IS YOUR GREATEST POWER!

My commitment to use this principle in my life is:

___

___

___

___

5. GO THE EXTRA MILE—WITH PMA

Render more and better service for which you are paid, and do it with a positive mental attitude. Form the habit of going the extra mile because of the pleasure you get out of it and because of what it does to you and for you deep down inside. It is inevitable that every seed of useful service you sow will multiply itself and come back to you in overwhelming abundance.

Following this principle will make you indispensable to other people. The principle manifests itself in most important laws: the Law of Compensation and the Law of Increasing Returns. These unvarying laws always reward intelligent effort rendered in the attitude of faith and rendered instinctively without regards to the limits of immediate compensation.

$$Q^1 + Q^2 + MA = C$$

The quality of the service rendered plus the quantity of the service rendered plus the mental attitude in which it is rendered equals your compensation in the world and the amount of space you will occupy in the hearts of your fellow man.

MAKE GOING THE EXTRA MILE WITH PMA A HABIT!

My commitment to use this principle in my life is:

___

6. CREATE PERSONAL INITIATIVE—WITH PMA

Personal initiative is the inner power that starts all action. It is the power that inspires the completion of that which one begins. It is the dynamo that starts the faculty of the imagination into action.

It is, in fact, self-motivation.

Motivation is that which induces action or determines choice. It is that which provides a motive. A motive is that inner urge only within the individual which incites you to action, such as an idea, an emotion, a desire or an impulse. It is a hope or other force which starts in an attempt to produce specific results.

When you know principles that can motivate you, you will then know principles that can motivate others.

Motivate yourself with PMA. Hope is the magic ingredient in motivation, but the secret of accomplishment is getting into action.

USE AND DEVELOP THE SELF-STARTER. DO IT NOW!

My commitment to use this principle in my life is:

7. BUILD A POSITIVE MENTAL ATTITUDE

PMA stands for 'positive mental attitude'.

A positive mental attitude is the right, honest, constructive thought, action or reaction to any person, situation or set of circumstances that does not violate the laws of God or the right of one's fellowman.

PMA allows you to build on hope and overcome the negative attitudes of despair and discouragement. It gives you the mental power, the feeling, the confidence to do anything you make up your mind to do. PMA is commonly referred to as the 'I can…I will' attitude applicable to all challenging circumstances in your life.

You create and maintain a positive mental attitude through your own willpower, based on motives of your own adaption. To develop PMA, strive to understand and apply the Golden Rule; be considerate and sensitive to the reactions of others; be sensitive to your own reactions by controlling your emotional responses; be a good finder; believe that any goal can be achieved; and develop what are understood to be right habits of thought and action.

A positive mental attitude is the catalyst necessary for achieving worthwhile success. Achievement is attained through some combination of PMA and definiteness of purpose with one or more of the other fifteen success principles.

MAINTAIN THE RIGHT ATTITUDE—A POSITIVE MENTAL ATTITUDE.

My commitment to use this principle in my life is:

_____

_____

8. CONTROL YOUR ENTHUSIASM—WITH PMA

A person without enthusiasm is like a watch without a mainspring. Father John O'Brien, research professor of theology at the University of Notre Dame, says, 'the first ingredient which I believe is absolutely necessary for a successful, efficient and competent individual is enthusiasm.' He adds, 'Enthusiasm comes from the Greek words that let you look into the root of this word—into its basic, fundamental and original meaning. The first is *theos*, which means God. The other two words are *en-Tae*, so that in the early usage of this term of the ancient Greeks, it literally meant, "God within you".' Further, 'No battle of any importance can be won without enthusiasm.'

To become enthusiastic about achieving a desirable goal, keep your mind on that goal day after day. The more worthy and desirable your objectives, the more dedicated and enthusiastic you will become. Understand and act on William James's statement, 'The emotions are not always immediately subject to reason but they are always immediately subject to ACTION' (emphasis added). Enthusiasm thrives on a positive mind and positive action. This is the key to controlling your enthusiasm: always give it a worthy goal to focus on and once you have channelled it toward that goal, it will carry you forward.

Real enthusiasm comes from within. However, enthusiasm is like getting water from a well; first you have to prime the pump but soon the water flows and flows and flows. You can be enthusiastic about everything and anything you know or do. Enthusiasm is a PMA characteristic. It can be generated naturally from one's thoughts, feelings and emotions, but more important, it can be generated at will.

TO BE ENTHUSIASTIC…ACT ENTHUSIASTICALLY!

My commitment to use the principle in my life is:

_____
_____
_____
_____

9. ENFORCE SELF-DISCIPLINE—WITH PMA

Self-discipline enables you to develop control over yourself. Self-discipline begins with mastery of your thoughts, what you really are, what you really do. Your failures and your successes are the results of habits. We are creatures of habit, but because we are minds with bodies, we can change our habits.

Self-discipline is perhaps the most important function in aiding an individual in the development and maintenance of habits of thought which enable that person to fix his or her entire attention upon any desired purpose and to hold it there until that purpose has been attained.

If you do not control your thoughts, you do not control your deeds. Think first and act afterward. Self-discipline is the principle by which you may voluntarily shape the patterns of your thoughts to harmonize with your goals and purposes.

DIRECT YOUR THOUGHTS, CONTROL YOUR EMOTIONS, ORDAIN YOUR DESTINY WITH PMA.

My commitment to use this principle in my life is:

_____
_____

10. THINK ACCURATELY—WITH PMA

Accurate thinking is based on two major fundamentals:

1. Inductive reasoning, based on the assumption of unknown facts or hypotheses.
2. Deductive reasoning, based on known facts or what are believed to be facts.

In school we are taught deductive and inductive reasoning and the fallacy that results in starting with the wrong premise in the one instance and making the wrong inference in the other. Accurate thinking and common sense are in part the result of experiences. You can learn from your own experiences as well as those of others when you learn how to recognize, relate, assimilate and apply principles in order to achieve your goals..

1. Separate facts from fiction or hearsay evidence.
2. Separate facts into classes: important and unimportant.

Be careful of others' opinions. They could be dangerous and destructive. Make sure your opinions are not someone else's prejudices. The accurate thinker learns to use his or her own judgment and to be cautious no matter who may endeavour to influence him or her.

TRUTH WILL BE TRUTH REGARDLESS OF A CLOSED MIND, IGNORANCE, OR REFUSAL TO BELIEVE.

My commitment to use this principle in my life is:

_____
_____
_____

11. CONTROL YOUR ATTENTION—WITH PMA

Controlled attention is organized mind power. It is the highest form of self-discipline. Controlled attention is the act of coordinating all the faculties of the mind and directing their combined power to a given end or definite objective. It is an act that can be obtained only by the strictest sort of self-discipline.

It is obvious, therefore, that when you voluntarily fix your attention upon a definite major purpose of a positive nature and force your mind through your daily habits of thought to dwell on the subject, you condition your subconscious mind to act on that purpose. Controlled attention, when it is focused upon the object of your definite major purpose, is a medium by which you make positive application of the principle of suggestion.

The mind never remains inactive, not even during sleep. It works continuously by reactions to the influences which reach it. Therefore, the object of controlled attention is that of keeping your mind busy with thought material which may be helpful in attaining the object of your desire.

Controlled attention is self-mastery of the highest order, for it is an accepted fact that the person who controls his or her own mind may control everything else.

KEEP YOUR MIND ON THE THINGS YOU WANT AND OFF THE THINGS YOU DON'T WANT.

My commitment to use this principle in my life is:

_____

12. INSPIRE TEAMWORK—WITH PMA

Teamwork is a willing cooperation and the coordination of effort to achieve a specific objective. When the spirit of teamwork is willing, voluntary and free, it leads to the attainment of great and enduring power.

It is a system which coordinates all the team players' resources and talents and automatically discourages dishonesty and unfairness, while it adequately compensates the individuals who serve honestly and unselfishly.

The principle of teamwork differs from the mastermind principle in that it is based on the coordination of effort without necessarily embracing the principle of definiteness of purpose or the principle of harmony, two important essentials of the mastermind.

Teamwork produces power, but the question of whether the power is temporary or permanent depends on the motive that inspired the cooperation. If the motive is one that inspires people to cooperate willingly, the power produced by this sort of teamwork will endure as long as that spirit of willingness prevails.

Teamwork builds individuals and businesses and provides unlimited opportunity for all. It is sharing a part of what you have—a part that is good—with others.

THAT WHICH YOU SHARE WILL MULTIPLY; THAT WHICH YOU WITHHOLD WILL DIMINISH.

My commitment to use this principle in my life is:

_____
_____
_____
_____

13. LEARN FROM ADVERSITY AND DEFEAT—WITH PMA

Every adversity carries with it the seed of an equivalent or greater benefit for those who have PMA and apply it.

Defeat may be a stepping-stone or a stumbling block, according to your mental attitude and how you relate it to yourself.

It is never the same as failure unless and until it has been accepted as such.

Your mental attitude in respect to defeat is the factor of major importance which determines whether you ride with tides of fortune or misfortune. The person with a positive metal attitude reacts to defeat in the spirit of determination not to accept it. The person with a negative mental attitude reacts to defeat in the spirit of hopeless acceptance.

THE WORST THING THAT HAPPENS TO YOU MAY BE THE BEST THING THAT CAN HAPPEN TO YOU IF YOU DON'T LET IT GET THE BEST OF YOU.

My commitment to use this principle in my life is:

_____
_____

14. CULTIVATE CREATIVE VISION—WITH PMA

Man's greatest gift is his thinking mind. It analyses, compares, chooses. It creates, visualizes, foresees and generates ideas.

Imagination is your mind's exercise, challenge and adventure. It is the key to all of a person's achievements, the mainspring of all human endeavour, the secret door to the soul of a person. Imagination inspires human endeavour in connection with material things and ideas associated with material things.

Imagination is the workshop of the human mind, where old ideas and established facts may be assembled into new combinations and put to new uses. It is the act of constructive intellect in the grouping of materials, knowledge or thoughts into new, original and rational systems, a constructive or creative faculty embracing poetic, artistic, philosophical, scientific and ethical imagination.

Creative vision may be an inborn quality of the mind or an acquired quality, for it may be developed by the free and fearless use of the faculty of imagination.

Creative vision extends beyond interest in material things. It judges the future by the past and concerns itself with the future more than with the past. Imagination is influenced and controlled by the powers of reason and experience. Creative vision pushes these aside and attains its ends by basically new ideas and methods.

One of the ways to increase your flow of ideas is by developing the habit of taking study time, thinking time, and planning time. Be quiet and motionless, and listen for that small, still voice that speaks from within as you contemplate the ways in which you can achieve your objectives.

WHAT CAN BE CONCEIVED CAN BE CREATED—WITH PMA.

My commitment to use this principle in my life is:

_____
_____
_____
_____

15. MAINTAIN SOUND HEALTH—WITH PMA

You are a mind with a body. Inasmuch as your brain controls your body, recognize that sound physical health demands a positive mental attitude, a health consciousness. Establish good, well-balanced health habits in work, play, rest, nourishment and study. To maintain a health consciousness, think in terms of good physical health, not in terms of illness or disease. Remember, what your mind focuses upon, your mind brings into existence, whether it is financial success or physical health.

To maintain a positive attitude for the development and the maintenance of a sound health consciousness, use self-discipline, keep your mind free of negative thoughts and influence and create and maintain a well-balanced life. Follow work with play, mental effort with physical effort, seriousness with humour, and you will be on the road to good health and happiness.

A sound mind and a sound body are attainable if you will put PMA to work for you. Remember, you can enjoy good health and live longer with PMA.

I FEEL HEALTHY! I FEEL HAPPY! I FEEL TERRIFIC!

My commitment to use this principle in my life is:

___

16. BUDGET YOUR TIME AND MONEY—WITH PMA

Intelligently balance your use of time and resources, both business and personal. Take inventory of yourself and your activities so that you discover where and how you are spending your time and your money.

Engage in study, thinking and planning time.

Don't waste your time or your money. Ten per cent of all you earn is yours to keep and invest. Like any good business, budget your money. Use your time wisely toward attainment of your objectives. Develop a plan for the use of your income for expenses, savings and investments.

YOU DON'T ALWAYS GET WHAT YOU EXPECT UNLESS YOU INSPECT—WITH PMA.

My commitment to use this principle in my life is:

___

17. USE COSMIC HABITFORCE—WITH PMA

Cosmic habitforce pertains to the entire universe and is the law by which the equilibrium of the universe is maintained through established patterns or habits. It is the law which forces every living creature and every particle of matter to come under the dominating influence of its environment, including the physical habits and thought habits of humankind.

Cosmic habitforces are the powers which you apply with PMA when you use the universal laws or principles. Cosmic habitforces are employed when you use your mind powers whether they pertain to your conscious or subconscious mind. That is how you think and grow richer or achieve anything in life you desire (in principle) that doesn't violate the laws of God or the rights of your fellowman.

All of us are ruled by habits. These are fastened upon us by repeated thoughts and experiences. You have complete right of control over your thoughts. We create patterns of thought by repeating certain ideas or behaviour until the Law of Cosmic Habitforce takes over those patterns and makes them more or less permanent unless or until you consciously rearrange them.

Habits: you have them—some good, perhaps others bad. Many you are aware of, but some that are undesirable you are blinded to. Each begins in your mind consciously or subconsciously. And each can be developed and neutralized or changed at will through the proper use of your mind. You have this power.

You are ruled by your habits. It takes a habit to replace a habit. Develop positive habits that will be in harmony with the achievement of your definite purpose or goal.

SOW AN ACT AND YOU REAP A HABIT.
SOW A HABIT AND YOU REAP A CHARACTER.
SOW A CHARACTER AND YOU REAP A DESTINY.

POINTS TO REMEMBER

1. Determine or fix in your mind exactly what you desire. Be definite.
2. Create mastermind alliances.
3. It is essential to develop a pleasing personality.

www.ingramcontent.com/pod-product-compliance
Lightning Source LLC
Chambersburg PA
CBHW021158160426
43194CB00007B/787